BLUEPRINTS
Maths Investigations

David and Wendy Clemson

Second edition

Stanley Thornes (Publishers) Ltd

Do you receive BLUEPRINTS NEWS?

Blueprints is an expanding series of practical teacher's ideas books and photocopiable resources for use in primary schools. Books are available for separate infant and junior age ranges for every core and foundation subject, as well as for an ever widening range of other primary teaching needs. These include **Blueprints Primary English** books and **Blueprints Resource Banks**. **Blueprints** are carefully structured around the demands of National Curriculum in England and Wales, but are used successfully by schools and teachers in Scotland, Northern Ireland and elsewhere.

Blueprints provide:
- Total curriculum coverage
- Hundreds of practical ideas
- Books specifically for the age range you teach
- Flexible resources for the whole school or for individual teachers
- Excellent photocopiable sheets – ideal for assessment and children's work profiles
- Supreme value.

Books may be bought by credit card over the telephone and information obtained on **(01242) 577944**. Alternatively, photocopy and return this **FREEPOST** form to receive **Blueprints News**, our regular update on all new and existing titles. You may also like to add the name of a friend who would be interested in being on the mailing list.

Please add my name to the **BLUEPRINTS NEWS** mailing list.

Mr/Mrs/Miss/Ms _____

Home address _____

_____ Postcode _____

School address _____

_____ Postcode _____

Please also send **BLUEPRINTS NEWS** to:

Mr/Mrs/Miss/Ms _____

Address _____

_____ Postcode _____

To: Marketing Services Dept., Stanley Thornes Ltd, FREEPOST (GR 782), Cheltenham, GL50 1BR

Text © David and Wendy Clemson 1993
Original line illustrations by Andrew Keylock © ST(P) Ltd 1993

The right of David and Wendy Clemson to be identified as authors of this work has been asserted by them in accordance with the Copyright, Designs and Patents Act 1988.

All rights reserved. No part of this publication may be reproduced or transmitted in any form or by any means, electronic or mechanical, including photocopy, recording or any information storage system, without permission in writing from the publisher or under licence from the Copyright Licensing Agency Limited. Further details of such licences (for reprographic reproduction) may be obtained from the Copyright Licensing Agency Limited, of 90 Tottenham Court Road, London W1P 9HE.

Material from the National Curriculum is Crown copyright and is reproduced with the permission of the Controller of Her Majesty's Stationery Office.

The publishers have made every effort to contact copyright holders and will be only too pleased to acknowledge anyone overlooked.

First published in 1993
Reprinted 1994
Second edition 1995
First published in new binding in 1998 by
Stanley Thornes (Publishers) Ltd
Ellenborough House
Wellington Street
CHELTENHAM GL50 1YW
England

A catalogue record for this book is available from the British Library.

ISBN 0–7487–3436–8

Typeset by Tech-Set, Gateshead, Tyne & Wear
Printed and bound in Great Britain by
Redwood Books, Trowbridge, Wiltshire

98 99 00 01 02 / 10 9 8 7 6 5 4 3 2 1

Contents

Introduction   iv

National Curriculum attainment target coverage   v

Record sheet   vi

Beginning investigations   1–3
i   Counts
ii   Left and Right
iii   Uni-, Bi-, Tri- and Quadr-
iv   Our Class Book of Records
v   Class Shop
vi   Holiday Money
vii   All About Us
viii   Copycats

Teacher's notes on the copymasters   4–31

Whole school investigations   32–3
A   Games Bonanza
B   School Maths Day
C   Doing Time
D   Data Day
E   Number Puzzles

Copymasters 1–85

Section 1: Levels 1/2
1   Measures 1
2   Making Faces
3   Counting Songs and Rhymes
4   Codes
5   Flick and Roller Books
6   Legs
7   3D Shapes in the Classroom
8   2D Shapes in the Classroom
9   Bear Race
10   Bus Sorts
11   Cross Stitch
12–15   Game Maker
16   Maze Game
17   Number Play
18   Pocket Sort
19   Road Signs
20   Shape Check
21   Tessellation: Bricks
22–3   Tessellation: Mosaic
24   Traffic Lights

Section 2: Levels 3/4
25   Town Map
26   Polyominoes
27   Möbius Band
28–9   Measures 2

30   Dominoes
31   24 Hours
32   Windscreen Wipers
33   Triangular Numbers
34   Square Numbers
35   Palindromes
36   Best Buy
37   Think of a Number
38   Story of 2
39   Questionnaire
40   Symmetry: Badges
41   Survey: Left and Right
42   Shapes in Buildings: Making a Trail
43   Prime Numbers
44–5   Mazes
46–7   Function Machines
48   Drinks Survey
49   Polybius Checkerboard Code
50   Finding out About Numbers
51   Calendar Month
52   Tangrams
53   Symmetry: Letters and Numerals
54–5   Tiles
56   9× Table and Dividing by 9
57   Addition Squares
58   Calculator Challenge
59   Magic Square

Section 3: Level 5
60   Pentagrams
61   Make a Newsletter
62   Furniture Design
63   Classroom Planner
64   Vedic Square
65–7   Pascal's Triangle
68–70   Fibonacci Series
71   Multiplication Squares and Patterns
72   Music by Chance
73   Angles
74   Euler's Relation
75   Handshakes
76   Tessellation: Pictures
77   Napier's Rods
78   Perimeter and Area
79   The Number 1089
80   Snooker

Section 4: Extension Investigations beyond Level 5
81–2   Networks
83   Knots
84   Celtic Knots
85   Plaiting

General Copymasters   a–d

Introduction

When we began to talk about what this book should contain we discussed again and again what we mean by a 'maths investigation'. We have settled for a definition which includes the following:

- At least to some extent it should include things children can do independently of the teacher
- It should not have one right answer
- It should lead children to think about what else they could do or find out using the same material, concepts or apparatus
- It should have some mathematical purpose but may include work beyond maths
- It may be related to 'real' problems of the everyday life sort but should also be fun to do for itself.

The Investigations that are in this book are, quite intentionally a 'mixed bag'. At the front of the book are some 'beginning investigations' for children at the start of their schooling. Investigations 1–24 are, in our opinion, predominantly for use with children in their infant years. 25–59 may be most useful to children in the middle years of their primary education. Investigations 60–85 are for children at the top end of the Primary school. The final section, Whole School Investigations, includes some examples of the kind of work that could be taken on by a whole school or department, culminating in an exhibition, presentation to parents, or open day for pupils from other schools.

Some Copymasters are record sheets for children; some are to stimulate discussion and motivate children and some are instruction sheets which help children to create things.

National Curriculum coverage

Alongside the text for each Investigation, and on the Copymasters you will find a reference to the Mathematics Attainment Targets to which the Investigation contributes. The Investigations are arranged in three main sections, each comprising Investigations which can be attempted at two Levels of the National Curriculum. Section One Investigations include work which is predominantly at Levels 1 and 2. Section Two Investigations correspond approximately to Levels 3 and 4, and Section Three broadly maps on to Level 5. Section Four comprises Extension Investigations beyond Level 5. A summary chart of the AT references for each Investigation appears on page v.

Using and Applying Mathematics

We have made no reference to Using and Applying Mathematics in the Investigations. The reason for this is that we believe investigative approaches to learning mean that children will do work which contributes to AT1 in all the Investigations in this book.

How to use this book

The Investigations in this book are numbered to correspond with the appropriate Copymasters. Within the text for each Investigation the 'Task in Action' notes are to give you, the teacher, a picture of what the children should be doing and how the Investigation should go. 'Teacher Help and Information' is intended to help you in offering support to the children and also in supplying additional or background information. 'Connections and Extensions' offer ways of joining the Investigation to others in the book and suggestions for directions the children's work can take. The general copymasters placed at the end of the book are referred to in the teacher's notes where essential. They are also intended as a valuable resource for all kinds of Maths Investigations. There is a record sheet on page vi which enables you to record which Investigations each child has tried.

National Curriculum attainment target coverage: summary chart

	AT2	AT3	AT4
Beginning investigations			
Counts	•		
Left and Right		•	
Uni-, Bi-, Tri- and Quadr	•		
Our Class Book of Records	•		
Class Shop	•		
Holiday Money	•		
All About Us	•		
Copycats	•		
Section 1: Levels 1/2			
Measures 1		•	
Making Faces	KS1		KS2
Counting Songs and Rhymes	•		
Codes	•		
Flick and Roller Books		•	
Legs	•		
3D Shapes in the Classroom		•	
2D Shapes in the Classroom		•	
Bear Race	•		
Bus Sorts	KS1		KS2
Cross Stitch		•	
Game Maker	KS1/2	KS1/2	KS2
Maze Game		•	
Number Play	•		
Pocket Sort	KS1		KS2
Road Signs		•	
Shape Check		•	
Tessellation: Bricks	•	•	
Tessellation: Mosaic	•	•	
Traffic Lights	•		
Section 2: Levels 3/4			
Town Map		•	
Polyominoes		•	
Möbius Band		•	
Measures 2		•	
Dominoes	•		•
24 Hours	•	•	
Windscreen Wipers	•	•	
Triangular Numbers	•		
Square Numbers	•		
Palindromes	•		
Best Buy	•		
Think of a Number	•		
Story of 2	•		
Questionnaire			•
Symmetry: Badges		•	
Survey: Left and Right	•	•	•
Shapes in Buildings: Making a Trail		•	

	AT2	AT3	AT4
Prime Numbers	•		
Mazes		•	
Function Machines	•		
Drinks Survey			•
Polybius Checkerboard Code	•		
Finding out about Numbers	•		
Calendar Month	•		
Tangrams		•	
Symmetry: Letters and Numerals		•	
Tiles		•	
9× Table and Dividing by 9	•		
Addition Squares	•		
Calculator Challenge	•		
Magic Square	•		
Section 3: Level 5			
Pentagram		•	
Make a Newsletter	•	•	
Furniture Design	•	•	
Classroom Planner	•	•	
Vedic Square	•	•	
Pascal's Triangle	•	•	•
Fibonacci Series	•	•	
Multiplication Squares and Patterns	•		
Music by Chance			•
Angles	•	•	
Euler's Relation	•	•	
Handshakes	•	•	•
Tessellation: Pictures		•	
Napier's Rods	•	•	
Perimeter and Area	•	•	
The Number 1089	•		
Snooker		•	
Section 4: Beyond Level 5			
Networks		•	
Knots		•	
Celtic Knots		•	
Plaiting		•	
Whole school investigations			
Games Bonanza	•	•	•
School Maths Day	•	•	•
Doing Time		•	
Data Day			•
Number Puzzles	•		

Record sheet

Child's Name: ———————   **Teacher's Initials** ———————

BEGINNING INVESTIGATIONS
i Counts
ii Left and Right
iii Uni-, Bi-, Tri- and Quadr-
iv Our Class Book of Records
v Class Shop
vi Holiday Money
vii All About Us
viii Copycats

SECTION 1: LEVELS 1/2
1 Measures 1
2 Making Faces
3 Counting Songs and Rhymes
4 Codes
5 Flick and Roller Books
6 Legs
7 3D Shapes in the Classroom
8 2D Shapes in the Classroom
9 Bear Race
10 Bus Sorts
11 Cross Stitch
12–15 Game Maker
16 Maze Game
17 Number Play
18 Pocket Sort
19 Road Signs
20 Shape Check
21 Tessellation: Bricks
22–3 Tessellation: Mosaic
24 Traffic Lights

SECTION 2: LEVELS 3/4
25 Town Map
26 Polyominoes
27 Möbius Band
28–9 Measures 2
30 Dominoes
31 24 Hours
32 Windscreen Wipers
33 Triangular Numbers
34 Square Numbers
35 Palindromes
36 Best Buy
37 Think of a Number
38 Story of 2
39 Questionnaire
40 Symmetry: Badges
41 Survey: Left and Right
42 Shapes in Buildings: Making a Trail
43 Prime Numbers
44–5 Mazes
46–7 Function Machines
48 Drinks Survey
49 Polybius Checkerboard Code
50 Finding out About Numbers
51 Calendar Month
52 Tangrams
53 Symmetry: Letters and Numerals
54–5 Tiles
56 9 × Table and Dividing by 9
57 Addition Squares
58 Calculator Challenge
59 Magic Square

SECTION 3: LEVEL 5
60 Pentagrams
61 Make a Newsletter
62 Furniture Design
63 Classroom Planner
64 Vedic Square
65–7 Pascal's Triangle
68–70 Fibonacci Series
71 Multiplication Squares and Patterns
72 Music by Chance
73 Angles
74 Euler's Relation
75 Handshakes
76 Tessellation: Pictures
77 Napier's Rods
78 Perimeter and Area
79 The Number 1089
80 Snooker

SECTION 4: EXTENSION INVESTIGATIONS BEYOND LEVEL 5
81–2 Networks
83 Knots
84 Celtic Knots
85 Plaiting

WHOLE SCHOOL INVESTIGATIONS
A Games Bonanza
B School Maths Day
C Doing Time
D Data Day
E Number Puzzles

Beginning investigations

Much of the work children do in their first three years of schooling may seem to them like 'investigating'. Teachers often try to create a working milieu in which children are active and influential in the course of their learning and in which there are a range of possible answers. Much invaluable investigating can be done without the children having to have the skill to record their work on a Copymaster. The Investigations that follow are a few examples of such Investigations. They require much teacher guidance and sometimes intervention to see the task through, but are no less invaluable than any of the other Investigations in the book.

AT 2 — i: Counts

Purpose
To alert children to the numbers all around them.

Resources
Access to all parts of the classroom and maybe other parts of school.

The task in action
Ask the children to find all the counts they can in the classroom. Make a class chart of the counts they make.

Teacher help and information
You may like to start them off by having a discussion about why we need to count things, and then make a suggested list of things that can be counted in the classroom. The list may run as follows: Girls, Boys, Red cardigans, Chairs, Tables, Registers, Rulers, Blue crayons, Rubbers, Books on animals, Doors, Windows....

A wall chart can spur further discussion about how many of some of the things are needed (for example, do we need more than 20 blue crayons, why do we need 30 chairs?)

Connections and extensions
Create a class number line and enter all the counts on it. Try counts in other parts of the school like the hall or cloakroom.

AT 3 — ii: Left and Right

Purpose
To help children identify left and right.

Resources
Roll of good quality lining paper, felt tip pen, crayons.

The task in action
Lay a child on their back on a large piece of paper. Draw round the child, cut out the outline and let them put in some features. Ask the children in turn to point to the left and right hands, arms, legs, feet and eyes. Turn the outline over and see if the children can identify left and right again. Cut out a number of child outlines and label parts of them left and right.

Teacher help and information
Mount the child outlines on the wall with some facing the wall and some with their backs to the wall so that children can stand against them and match, for example, their hands and feet to those on display.

Connections and extensions
Let the children look at themselves in a mirror and talk about left and right on the 'mirror person'. Then let the children draw themselves on a piece of paper, mark in left and right, play with a plastic mirror and talk about what happens to their picture.

AT 2 — iii: Uni-, Bi, Tri and Quadr-

Purpose
To alert children to the idea that there are sometimes number clues in words, and to look for examples.

Resources
Pictures of some of the following: unicycle, universe, bicycle, binoculars, bikini, tricycle, triceratops, triangle, quadruped.

The task in action
See which things children can identify from the pictures. Discuss the meanings of the words. Help the children to find, draw and label some more.

Teacher help and information
Make a class book in which these can be the first entries.

Connections and extensions
Start with words that are familiar to some of the children and let them learn more. They may delight in knowing what a quintet, a centenary, a decade a quadrangle, or unisex means.

iv: Our Class Book of Records

AT 2

Purpose
To find out, by making comparisons, who in the class holds the current 'record' in a variety of ways.

Resources
A 'Guiness Book of Records', strips of paper or string to help with measuring comparisons.

The task in action
Help the children to generate a list of things they would like to establish a record in. These might include some they can establish with chalk marks on a floor or wall, or using string; for example, who has:

- the longest reach
- longest stride
- shortest foot
- longest thumb.

Some that are counts, for example who can:

- bounce a ball most times
- stand on one leg for longest while counting;

and those that are determined by collecting and sifting information, like who:

- has the most pets
- gets up earliest
- has the longest name.

Teacher help and information
Once the children begin to devise their own records, it may be appropriate to see if everyone can have an entry!

Connections and extensions
This could be extended to include a parallel class, offering important number and measuring comparisons.

v: Class Shop

AT 2

Purpose
To find out all the maths involved in shopping.

Resources
Classroom shop; items for sale may be things the children have made or old greeting cards and food packaging; a till, play money, shopping bags, purses.

The task in action
Offer the children challenges over a number of sessions. They can include things like:

- What can you buy for 10p? What else?
- How much do you need to buy two items?
- What is the cheapest/most expensive thing in the shop?
- What do you get when you give the shopkeeper money?
- How does the shopkeeper have money of his own?
- Where do we get cash?

Teacher help and information
Children need to investigate equivalence, the idea of a 'good buy', change and exchange.

Connections and extensions
The children need to practise playing shop in a variety of settings within the class, and a post office, supermarket, play dough fruit shop and toy shop are a few suggestions for making the setting renewable and fresh.

The work can be extended by exploring what a plastic card and cheque are, how banks work, and some of the ways to save and invest.

vi: Holiday Money

AT 2

Purpose
To explore the kinds of units used in a variety of currencies including our own.

Resources
A set of British coins and notes to include at least the following: 1p, 2p, 5p, 10p, 20p, 50p, £1 and a £5 note; a variety of foreign coins and notes.

The task in action
Let the children look at the range of British coins and notes, with the naked eye and under magnifiers. Talk about our currency and, for example the number of pence in a pound. Look at a variety of foreign currencies, do drawings and rubbings, and talk about the names for the coins and notes, and their worth.

Teacher help and information
Invite the children to bring in coins that are left over from holidays or are part of a coin collection. Ask your colleagues to look for coins at home. Experiment with coin rubbings and see if they can be enlarged on the photocopier.

Connections and extensions
Link this work to the Investigation entitled Class Shop above.

vii: All About Us

AT 2

Purpose
To introduce children to the idea that information can be collected, 'stored' and communicated systematically.

Resources
To be decided in consultation with the children; though large sheets of paper, and felt tip pens may also be useful.

The task in action

Plan an assembly or presentation that the whole class can make to another class, the whole school, their parents, or a student or new teacher joining the school. Discuss with the children what information they want to give their audience about themselves. Talk to the children about possible ways of collecting it, sorting it out and 'telling' it. Decide on the body of information to be collected, let the children get their presentation ready.

Teacher help and information

You may be able to give the children help in being systematic. For example, if they have a tally chart, lined paper or a list of the names of everyone in the class, this may help information collection. A tape recorder may also be useful.

A plan for quick information collection may include large sheets of paper displayed around the room. Write on each of these a category of information the children wish to collect; for example, 'How many brothers have you?' and a child can write in the possible groups, maybe None, 1, 2, 3, 4 or more. The children can then all tour the room and write their name, initials, or draw their face in the appropriate places on each information sheet. The children can then decide as a class what happens to the information next.

Connections and extensions

Join forces with another class and make some data comparisons.

AT 2

viii: Copycats

Purpose

To give the chldren the opportunity to invent patterns and sequences and 'translate' them from one medium to another.

Resources

As wide a variety of the following as you can muster: art materials, including paint, felt tips, printing materials, clay, plasticine; percussion and other musical instruments; poems and rhymes that offer 'repeats' like rounds or songs where words are added each time it is sung (*The Twelve Days of Christmas* is an example); construction toys.

The task in action

Ask the children to create a pattern of their own, using an art medium or construction toys. They may decide on something like one of the patterns shown here:

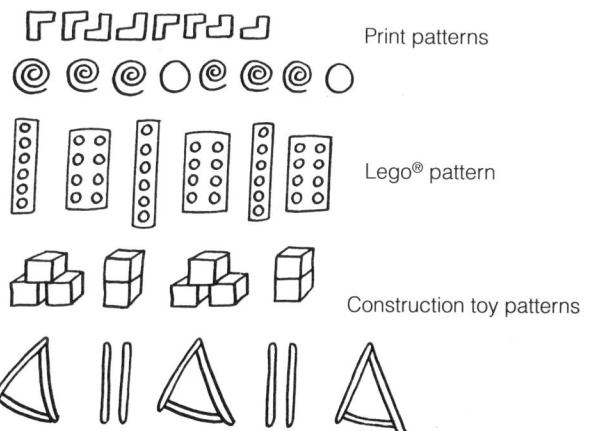

Then invite them to 'translate' that same pattern into a model, or percussion, or words, or numbers. Display a variety of patterns and let all the children look for the sequences.

Teacher help and information

Encourage the children to make their 'starter sequence' simple, so that they can replicate it easily.

Connections and extensions

Link this work to all that the children do in relation to counting, number lines and ordering.

Section 1: Levels 1/2

C1: Measures 1
AT 3

Purpose
To introduce the idea that a measuring tool should be appropriate for the purpose.

Resources
Lolly sticks, string, a wide variety of objects to measure.

The task in action
The children have to identify and draw objects which they believe are best measured by one of the non-standard measures on the Copymaster. To do this they need to have access to as wide a range of objects as possible, from which they can choose those they consider appropriate. They can compare and discuss their choices.

Teacher help and information
The idea of there being appropriate measuring instruments for different measuring jobs is very important for the children to develop. They will then find it easier to understand the idea that instruments using standard measures have limited applicability, depending on ease of use and degree of accuracy required. The history of measurement begins with the use of non-standard measures and to take children from these to standard ones seems to help in their understanding of why we need standard measures and why we have a range of such measures available.

Connections and extensions
This investigation links to number-line work, (for example, strides across the room make a stride number line) and beginning fractions, (prompting discussions of comparisons like, 'Is it half as wide? Half as long?')
See also Investigations 28/29: Measures 2.

C2: Making Faces
KS1 AT2 KS2 AT4

Purpose
To practise sorting and tallying.

Resources
Scissors.

The task in action
The child has to cut out the collection of eyes, noses and ears, and put them on the face. The challenge is for them to find out the greatest number of different faces that they can make using the two pairs of eyes and ears and the two noses.

Teacher help and information
If the child goes on trying combinations of attributes at random suggest ways of being more methodical and show how to tally the combinations of features used. One way of doing this would be to set out a table for combinations of, say nose and eyes whilst keeping the same pair of ears.

EARS1	NOSE 1	NOSE 2
EYES1	E1,N1	E1,N2
EYES2	E2,N2	E2,N2

A similar table for EAR 2 will show that, with two pairs of eyes and ears and two noses, there are eight possible different faces.

Connections and extensions
Ask the children to try drawing and cutting out another nose (or pair of eyes or ears) and see how many more faces they can make. What if there were three possible pairs of eyes and ears and three noses?
See also Investigation 10: Bus Sorts and Investigation 18: Pocket Sorts.

C3: Counting Songs and Rhymes
AT 2

Purpose
To use songs and rhymes to support an understanding of counts and counting.

Resources
Music and poetry books and anthologies which contain lots of songs and rhymes.

The task in action
The rhymes on the Copymaster can be used in the following ways:

- as starting points for discussing number in rhymes,
- as starting rhymes for a class collection,
- as starting points for individual children to make a rhyme book.

Teacher help and information
Rhyme books can be used by younger children or given away to younger relatives as gifts by the children who made them. The three rhymes on the Copymaster are well-known traditional nursery rhymes.

When compiling rhymes and songs remember to include playground chants.

Connections and extensions
This work, if done by the class, could form the basis of a class assembly in which the theme of the use of counting and numbers could be explored. Extend the work to take in traditional counting rhymes from other cultures.

Link this work to Investigation 38: The Story of Two, and Investigation 50: Finding out about Numbers.

AT 2 — C4: Codes

Purpose
To use some examples of codes to generate ideas on pattern, sequencing and communication.

Resources
Books about the use of codes including Semaphore and Morse.

The task in action
The child is asked to look carefully at the Semaphore and Morse codes for numbers, which are presented on the Copymaster. They are then invited to invent their own number code and set number challenges for classmates.

Teacher help and information
Encourage the children to look for the pattern in the codes presented. Ask them to write, for example, their own house number or telephone number in Semaphore and Morse. For additional practice they could sign them, using two arms for semaphore and taps on a hard surface or percussion instrument for Morse.

Connections and extensions
Let the children look for other codes and play with them. One example is Braille.

Link this to Investigation 49: Polybius Checkerboard Code.

AT 3 — C5: Flick and Roller Books

Purpose
To explore space ideas through simple animation.

Resources
Strips of cartridge or other heavyweight papers for children to make more flick and roller books when they have used the Copymaster.

The task in action
The Copymaster has page outlines for two types of animation. The flick book should be made from a series of drawings, one on each page of the book, which represent snapshots of an action. Here is an example set:

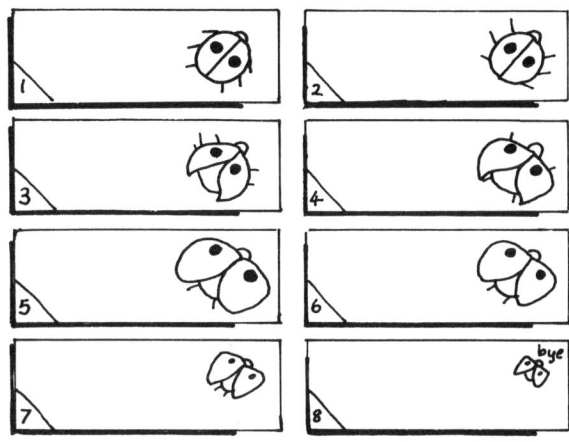

Flick book

The child has to draw a rough idea on paper and then transfer it, frame by frame, to the Copymaster. Staple the ends of each of the drawings together and flick through, as rapidly as possible. This will give an animated effect.

The second part of the Copymaster offers a 'roller' book. Here the child draws two pictures only of the same thing but in a different position. Here is an example:

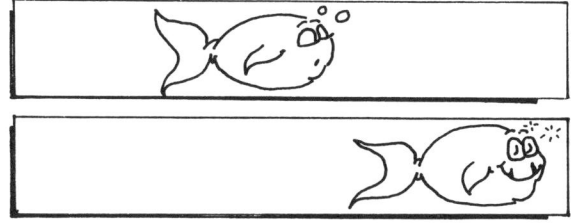

Roller book

Staple the left hand ends together and roll a pencil up loosely in the top page. Then move the pencil end so that the page unrolls. Then move the pencil rapidly back and forth along the top sheet and the top and bottom drawings can be seen in rapid succession. This will cause an illusion of movement.

Teacher help and information
Remind the children that for best effect in the flick book the change in the picture from one page to the next should be small. In making up flick and roller books it is important that the sheets are lined up as precisely as possible. It helps to have each sheet cut out very carefully. It is useful to trim the free ends of the pages of the flick book after stapling. Experiment with the staples on the right for some books to see if it makes it easier for left handed children.

Connections and extensions
Cartoons and animation effects are very familiar to children. Use their experience to explore how these effects are obtained. This discussion should include ideas to do with movement, relative size and the characteristics which allow rapid recognition of objects and animals. This could lead into a consideration of the art of cartoon drawing as well as the production of comic strips.

AT 2 | C6: Legs

Purpose
To encourage children to investigate patterns based on counting in twos, that is the even numbers.

Resources
Reference books about the animal world.

The task in action
The child has to draw an animal which will fit each category based on numbers of legs.

Teacher help and information
Counting in twos and the beginnings of discussion about even numbers is supported by this Investigation.

Connections and extensions
This work can be linked to ideas on:

- pairs and other number names
- the idea of even numbers
- the development of times table work
- symmetry.

See also Investigation 38: The Story of 2, Investigation 40: Symmetry: Badges, and Investigation 53: Symmetry: Letters and Numerals.

AT 3 | C7: 3D Shapes in the Classroom

Purpose
To find, match and draw 3D shapes in the classroom.

Resources
Access to all parts of the classroom

The task in action
The child has to find something in the classroom that matches each of the shapes on the Copymaster and draw those things in the right shape outline.

Teacher help and information
Let a group of children do this activity, each child having a copy of the Copymaster. To avoid replication they should do the task at different times. Label their drawings for them. You or the children can cut around their shapes and add them to a group shape set. Discuss which shapes are most common in class. If the children are unsure about the shapes they can continue to match without naming for a number of sessions. Then you can give them the shape names.

Connections and extensions
Take the children round other parts of the school to spot shapes. Let the children work in pairs to list or draw all the different examples they can find that are a given shape. Assemble these to show which shapes are common.

See also Investigation 20: Shape Check, and Investigation 42: Shapes in Buildings: Making a Trail.

AT 3 | C8: 2D Shapes in the Classroom

Purpose
Matching and naming 2D shapes in the classroom.

Resources
Access to all parts of the classroom.

The task in action
The child has to find things around the room that have faces matching the shapes on the Copymaster and draw an appropriate example object within each shape outline.

Teacher help and information
Let a group of children do this activity, each child having a copy of the Copymaster. To avoid replication they should do the task at different times. Label their drawings for them. You or the children can cut around their shapes and add them to a group shape set. Discuss which shapes are most common in class. If the children are unsure about the shapes they can continue to match without naming for a number of sessions. Then you can give them the shape names.

Connections and extensions
Link this work to Investigation 7: 3D Shapes in the classroom, Investigation 19: Road Signs, Investigation 20: Shape Check, and Investigation 42: Shapes in Buildings: Making a Trail.

AT 2 | C9: Bear Race

Purpose
To practise naming numbers and counting, to learn about game playing and maths involved in making and playing games.

Resources
Die, counters or buttons to use as playing pieces.

The task in action
The children can work in pairs to play the game as a simple track, discuss the pattern of play and try modifying the game.

Teacher help and information
The intention is, not only to give the children chances to play a simple game, but to begin to talk about the nature of games and how they are made. Encourage the children to speculate about their game. Some challenges appear on the Copymaster. See if the children can generate some more.

Connections and extensions
If the children become skilled at analysing what their game involves, you may like to show them commercially produced games that they can try and comment on. Talk about the 'rules for being a good player' as opposed to 'playing to win' and whether different games need different kinds of skill.
See also Investigations 12, 13, 14, 15: Game Maker.

| KS1 AT2 |
| KS2 AT4 | **C10: Bus Sorts**

Purpose
To use logic to determine patterns of using four colours.

Resources
Wax crayons or coloured pencils.

The task in action
The child can use the colours prescribed to fill in the bus outlines on the Copymaster in a variety of ways.

Teacher help and information
The Copymaster does not allow space for all possible combinations of colours. If several children do this task, you may be able to amass from their total work, an example of each of the colourways. There are 24 possible combinations. To help to see this the bus can be viewed as being three horizontal strips and one vertical strip.

Connections and extensions
Link this work to Investigation 2: Making Faces and Investigation 18: Pocket Sort.

Teacher help and information
Children may need help to devise a design simple enough to be recognisable when done in crosses. Close supervision is mandatory, as is advice about keeping needles, even when attached to thread, well away from faces.

Connections and extensions
This work could be extended into a discussion of tessellation. See Investigation 21: Tessellation: Bricks, and Investigation 22, 23: Tessellation: Mosaics.

| AT 3 | **C11: Cross Stitch**

Purpose
To enable children to invent, design and construct a picture involving a pattern of stitches, and in the course of this to practise translating shapes and making counts.

Resources
Binca fabric or card and dotty paper (General Copymaster e is dotty squares), sewing thread and blunt needles, scissors, squared paper (General Copymaster a is 5 mm squares).

The task in action
The child is asked to draw some rough pictures on the Copymaster and transfer one of these to squared paper. The design can then be sewn on Binca® or dotty or squared paper placed on card, using the squared paper drawing as a pattern.

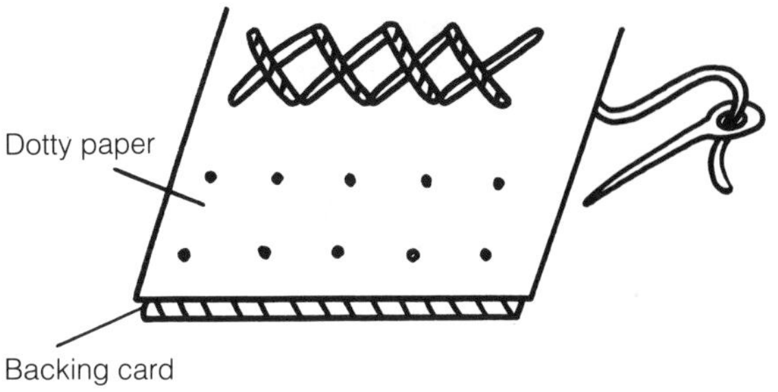

| KS1 AT2,3 |
| KS2 AT2,3,4 | **C12–15: Game Maker**

Purpose
To give children the chance to invent and modify games of their own, and give practice in 'game skills' like prediction, counting and logic.

Resources
Card, felt-tips, coloured pencils and crayons, spent matches and dice or spinners.

The task in action
The child is asked to invent a game using either the game track on Copymaster 12 or the game board on Copymaster 13. Copymasters 14 and 15 have some example playing pieces, illustrations and 'challenge spots' that can be coloured, cut out and stuck down on the game. Children can also embellish the games with their own ideas.

7

Teacher help and information
Each child may want to make their own game, but if they work in pairs and use two base boards, they may fuel each other's thinking as well as being able to test play the games. Encourage the children to invent some challenges for each square they put a star or a Wham! on.

Connections and extensions
As in the Connections and extensions to Investigation 9: Bear Race, if the children become skilled at analysing what their game involves, you may like to show them commercially produced games that they can try and comment on. Talk about the 'rules for being a good player' as opposed to 'playing to win' and whether different games need different kinds of skill.

| AT 3 | **C16: Maze Game** |

Purpose
To allow children to begin to work on direction, movement and networks.

Resources
Scissors, glue to stick down the dragons (if the children wish).

The task in action
The child is asked to find routes across and down the length of the maze, and find a really long route through. They can then block some paths with the dragons and explore other routes.

Teacher help and information
The intention is to get children using shape and space and prediction skills to 'play' with a simple maze. The 'walls' and pathways have been deliberately made of similar widths in some places to make the maze a little more challenging.

Connections and extensions
Having used the maze on the Copymaster the children can go on to draw their own, or make the challenges more difficult for their classmates.
  See also Investigation 44, 45: Mazes.

| AT 2 | **C17: Number Play** |

Purpose
To encourage children to see numbers as fun, and to 'play' at generating them.

Resources
Counting aids.

The task in action
The child is asked to make big and small numbers and several additions from a selection of numerals.

Teacher help and information
This is an opportunity to allow children to explore numbers without having the numerals in 'order' placed before them. For those children who are unsure about place value, the numbers they record can be within their understanding; others may be ready to consider thousands, hundreds, tens and units.

Connections and extensions
Give the children the numerals 6, 7, 8, 9 and 0 and ask them to repeat the challenges. Invite them to create a little book of *Things to do with numbers 1–5*.

This work links to all Investigations using numbers.

| KS1 AT2 KS2 AT4 | **C18: Pocket Sort** |

Purpose
To practise sorting using a variety of criteria.

Resources
Possibly the real items that appear on the Copymaster, to set out on a card pocket outline.

The task in action
The child is asked to sort the contents of the pocket on the Copymaster in as many ways as they can. They then add a new item to the pocket and see how it affects subsequent sorts.

Teacher help and information
It may help the child's sorts if they can handle and move the items they are sorting around, so you may decide to replicate the items on the Copymaster with the real things. Encourage the children to be imaginative in their sorts, which may include things like:

- what it is made from
- natural or man made
- edible
- colour
- shape
- where used
- can be played with
- 'go together' because …

Connections and extensions
Link this work to Investigation 2: Making faces, and Investigation 10: Bus sorts.

C19: Road Signs
AT 3

Purpose
To provoke children's awareness of shapes around them and to alert them to common signs and symbols.

Resources
The children need to walk around the locality, looking for road signs.

The task in action
The child is required to fill in road sign pictures to fit the appropriate outline shapes on the Copymaster.

Teacher help and information
Help the children with their observation and interpretive skills. Some common road signs that children may spot include:

Signs giving orders (mostly circular)

maximum speed   no cycling   school crossing patrol

Warning signs (mostly triangular)

school   pedestrian crossing   crossroads

Information signs (all rectangular)

hospital ahead   parking   no through road

Connections and extensions
This work can be extended by looking at the shapes of other signs and symbols in common use, for example, signs for danger, poison, avoid litter and recycle.
See also Investigation 4: Codes, and Investigation 8: 2D Shapes in the Classroom.

C20: Shape Check
AT 3

Purpose
To explore some of the characteristics of 3D shapes.

Resources
A wide variety of 3D shapes, found, for example, in packaging, maths apparatus and toys.

The task in action
Using a collection of a variety of shapes, the child is required to test them to see whether they pack, stack, roll and what they may be used for.

Teacher help and information
Let every child try out their predictions about the characteristics of the shapes, and 'play' until they are convinced of their findings. The uses of shapes provides discussion and sets of shape books can be drawn for display and used as a classroom resource.

Connections and extensions
Extend this work by asking the children to talk about or draw some constructions or machines that they invent. Ask them to justify their use of shapes.
Link this work to Investigation 7: 3D shapes in the classroom.

C21: Tessellation: Bricks
AT 2, 3

Purpose
To identify, replicate and create patterns from shapes that tessellate.

Resources
Toy building blocks which are cuboid; brick walls and buildings to look at or photographs of these.

The task in action
Using the brick as a familiar shape the child has to try to create different tessellating patterns of this shape. If possible take the children out to look at buildings and brick-walls and photograph them.

Teacher help and information
What is important is that the children can see that, in outline, there are three differently proportioned faces each of which occur twice as opposite faces.

9

Connections and extensions
Explore the variety of brick patterns in use in the building industry and find out their names.

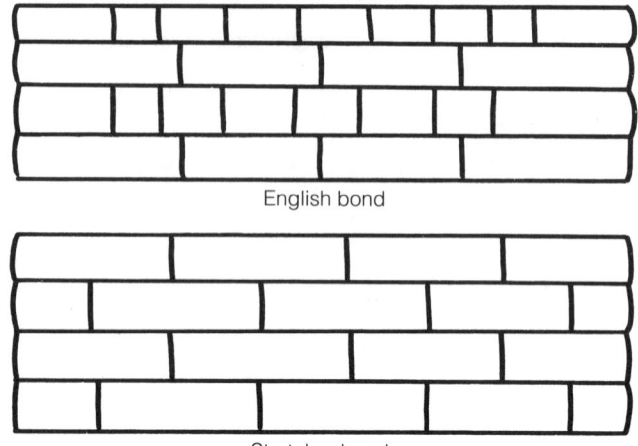

English bond

Stretcher bond

See also Investigation 22, 23: Tessellation: Mosaic.

C22, 23: Tessellation: Mosaic
AT 3

Purpose
To identify which of a variety of shapes tessellate, and which tessellate when used together with another shape, through play with mosaics.

Resources
Paints, felt-tips, coloured pencils or wax crayons, scissors, backing paper and glue.

The task in action
The child has to cut out the shapes on Copymaster 22, try placing them together without gaps in between, and record what they find out on Copymaster 23.

Teacher help and information
The theoretical understanding of tessellation should be tackled at an advanced Level. Children working at Levels 1 and 2, however, enjoy pattern making and can, without discussing the theory at this stage, make successful examples of tessellating patterns. Squares, equilateral triangles and regular hexagons tessellate as do irregular shapes with internal angles adding up to 360°. There are eight possible 'semi-regular' tessellations (where two shapes are used). These include octagons and squares, and squares with equilateral triangles.

Connections and extensions
Show the children some of the work of M. C. Escher. Look for tessellating shapes in the environment.
See also Investigation 21: Tessellation: Bricks.

C24: Traffic Lights
AT 2

Purpose
To alert children to important sequences around them.

Resources
The children need, if possible, to see the sequence at some traffic lights, and a pelican crossing. If there are none near school, find out if a road safety video shows this information. Torches, coloured cellophane and tissue may also be useful.

The task in action
The child is asked to colour the lights on sequences for traffic lights and a pelican crossing.

Teacher help and information
To reinforce these light sequences, which may prove vital in ensuring children's safety on the road, cover the ends of three torches with red, green and yellow sweet wrappers, and make red and green tissue 'pedestrians'. Torches can be switched on behind these at the appropriate times, or on and off to 'flash'. Let the children have goes at practising and watching the sequences.

Connections and extensions
Extend this work by discussing other sequences in everyday life. Examples may include the following:
- before school routines
- the pattern of the school day
- patterns of growth or metamorphosis in living things
- seasons
- how to use a lift, buy a railway ticket, buy sweets or a drink from a machine, programme a washing machine or toy robot.

Link this work to Investigations 3: Counting Songs and Rhymes, and Investigation 4: Codes.

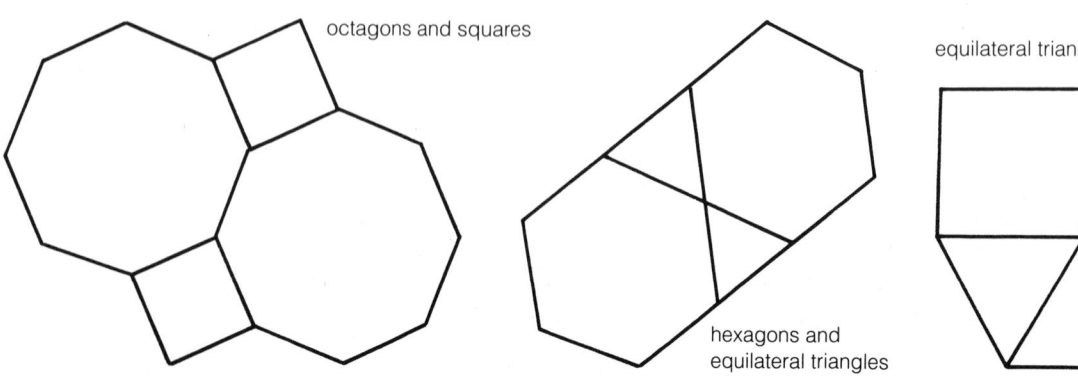

octagons and squares

hexagons and equilateral triangles

equilateral triangles and squares

Section 2: Levels 3/4

C25: Town Map
AT 2, 3

Purpose
To use co-ordinates to develop a guide to exploring a location.

Resources
Town and city guidebooks and maps.

The task in action
The children are asked to devise unique town guides. Having done so they can compare their efforts with those of others and use this to evaluate the merits of different strategies and approaches.

Teacher help and information
Tell the children that co-ordinates are in common use for the production and interpretation of town guides. They are commonly of the type which offer the identification of an area and use letters and numbers. For the more accurate pin-pointing of location numbers are used as grid references. Cartesian co-ordinates are so-called after René Descartes (1596–1650), the French philosopher and mathematician.

Connections and extensions
The children could add a scale and compass directions to their map, and write some distances and compass directions into their guide.

There are many board and computer games now which make use of co-ordinates. Bring some of these into the classroom for the children to explore.

See also Investigation 68, 69: Networks.

C26: Polyominoes
AT 3

Purpose
To explore patterns of shape and number.

Resources
One inch squared paper (General Copymaster b is one inch squared), scissors.

The task in action
The child has to assemble as many pentominoes cut from squared paper as they can, record how many and fold them to see which would make an open box. They are then asked to do the same tasks to produce hexominoes.

Teacher help and information
Tell the children that polyominoes are figures which are produced by joining squares, so that they touch along at least one edge. Pentominoes have five squares and there are 12 different combinations of five squares. The addition of an extra square produces hexominoes of which there are 35.

Connections and extensions
Introduce the children to dominoes, made from two squares, and trominoes made from three. There are different numbers of unique combinations that can be made depending upon the number of squares chosen as the basic set.

The full list is:

Shape	Number of squares	Total combinations
Domino	2	1
Tromino	3	2
Tetromino	4	5
Pentomino	5	12
Hexomino	6	35

Connect this work to the construction of regular 3D shapes and the nets of these.

The children can also try using equilateral triangles rather than squares. These are called polyiamonds with the diamond made up of two triangles being the best known.

See also Investigation 42: Shapes in Buildings: Making a Trail.

C27: Möbius Band
AT 3

Purpose
To explore and try to predict phenomena about surfaces by making and cutting bands of paper.

Resources
Scissors, 5 mm squared paper (General Copymaster a is 5 mm squares), Sellotape®, wax crayons.

The task in action
The children need to cut strips of paper of a constant width of the dimensions given on the Copymaster, and then stick and cut them as instructed. Care has to be taken to align the ends of the strips for sticking together. Squared paper has been suggested because it enables the children to follow a line when cutting. The strips can be longer than suggested (28 cm can be cut from an A4 sheet).

Teacher help and information
The Möbius Band has only one surface! Such bands are used in belt driven machinery in order to maximise the life of a belt as the whole surface is used rather than one side. The Möbius band is named after the German mathematician, August Ferdinand Möbius (1790–1868), noted for his work in geometry and topology.

Connections and extensions
Take the children to see some belt driven machinery. Machinery like this can be seen in many working museums, both industrial and agricultural. Show the children some reproductions of the work of the artist M. C. Escher who used the Möbius Band in his paintings and drawings. Escher is also well known for his use of tessellation and his pictures can provoke discussion about optical effects and illusions.
 See also Investigation 81, 82: Networks.

AT 3 | C28, C29: Measures 2

Purpose
To choose appropriate measures and measuring instruments to help solve problems.

Resources
None are mandatory, but if the children want to match their solutions to actual objects, they can help find them.

The task in action
The children can be offered a choice from the problems (there are two Copymasters 28 and 29) or you could give one each to different groups of children so that they can feed back their suggestions to the others.

Teacher help and information
Each of the problems offered is amenable to extensive experiment and analysis, and the most important help the children may need is in not blocking ideas and ways of thinking early in their discussions.

Connections and extensions
The children can add to the list of problems by inventing some to challenge their classmates. They can help to collect the actual dimensions of a variety of objects that may appear as measurement problems and set this data alongside the outcomes of classroom discussion to promote discussion about measures and instruments.
 The children can also look at sizing ranges and work out, for example, the range of sizes and the average or optimum size of, for example, the following:

- cycling helmets to fit everyone in the class
- exercise books
- lunch boxes
- trays, or drawers for individual children to store their equipment in class.

AT 2, 4 | C30: Dominoes

Purpose
To explore a set of dominoes for number patterns; the addition of numbers and the development of a distribution.

Resources
Set of dominoes, squared paper (General Copymasters b and c are squared papers).

The task in action
The child should count the number of dominoes in a set and then sum the total number of dots on each domino and tally how many dominoes have dots of each total between 0 and 12.

Teacher help and information
The numbers of dominoes with each dot total can be used to produce a block graph to show the pattern of distribution.

Connections and extensions
Dominoes offer a range of opportunities spanning addition, subtraction and number comparisons (e.g. Odds and Evens). Encourage the children to arrange the dominoes logically in order to see patterns. For example, they might record the domino set as:

6-6	6-5	6-4	6-3	6-2	6-1	6-0
5-5	5-4	5-3	5-2	5-1	5-0	
4-4	4-3	4-2	4-1	4-0		
3-3	3-2	3-1	3-0			
2-2	2-1	2-0				
1-1	1-0					
0-0						

 This investigation can be extended in a variety of ways, including these:

- explore a grid like the one above in relation to the first and second numbers in columns and diagonals
- in the grid there are 7 dominoes in the first row, 6 in the second and so on. The totals of the rows adds up to the total number of dominoes in a set, but it is also the sum of the consecutive whole numbers 1–7 inclusive. Use the Connections and extensions in Investigation 33: Triangular Numbers to explore the summing of consecutive whole numbers
- invent domino sets which have more than 6 dots in one half. How many will there be - bearing in mind what is known about the sum of consecutive whole numbers?
- total the number of dots in a domino set and divide this by the number of dominoes. Why is that the average? If you increase the size of the set what will be the new average?

| AT 3 | **C31: 24 Hours** ▷ |

Purpose
To help children acquire a concept of time by looking at how their activities fit a 24-hour pattern and are cyclical.

Resources
Play clock face, digital clock.

The task in action
The children have to draw, on the copymaster, some of the activities that they regularly do over a 24-hour time period. They then cut out the 12-hour strips and glue them to make a cylinder, showing all 24 hours. This can then be rotated. They can look at one another's daily pattern of life.

Teacher help and information
Remind the children of the pattern of the hours over a 24-hour period, using the play clock face and the 'time forward' button on the digital clock. Help the children look for similarities in their daily patterns, like lunch time; and differences, like bedtimes.

Connections and extensions
Use the children's efforts as a starting point for daily routines data-collection and analysis. For example, the children could record their dad's and mum's day pattern, revealing shift or night work.

More detailed data about daily activities could be collected and collated to start a discussion about the modal averages of time spent in, for example, sleeping, watching television, reading, and playing.

| AT 2, 3 | **C32: Windscreen Wipers** ▷ |

Purpose
To investigate concepts to do with arcs, angles and area.

Resources
Measuring tapes, string, squared paper (General Copymaster b is 1 inch squares), and/or other resources that the children decide they need.

The task in action
The challenge is for the children to establish the efficiency of windscreen wipers in relation to the area of the windscreen. They will need to estimate or measure the length of the wiper blade or blades and the area of the screen. They will also need to find out what amount of rotation is involved in the movement of the blades. If it is possible, the children could also ask the car owners for a subjective rating of the windscreen wiper efficiency on their car.

Teacher help and information
Because of the aerodynamic design of many modern cars the size of the screen can appear quite different from that established by measurement. The length of a blade is close to the height of the screen, but it must also have a relationship to the width of the screen. Some cars have one wiper blade close to the centre of the screen. Discuss the efficacy of having one or two blades.

Connections and extensions
Windscreen wipers come in a range of sizes intended for named cars. The children could use their findings to predict sizes of windscreens. These could be checked with the help of windscreen replacement companies or auto spare suppliers who might be willing to let you have copies of car-handbooks and catalogues. Repair manuals found in the public library may also yield wiper information.

The car industry is made up of a variety of small manufacturers supplying components to the large car manufacturer. The children could investigate what might happen to wiper manufacturing firms if there is, for example, a reduction in car sales, the life of all parts has to be guaranteed for five years, or a big car manufacturing plant is closed.

See also Investigation 78: Perimeter and Area.

| AT 2 | **C33: Triangular Numbers** ▷ |

Purpose
To explore number patterns which are useful in number work and in algebra.

Resources
Counters, triangular dotty paper (General Copymaster d).

The task in action
Check that the child understands that all counters (with the exception of the one set down at the start) should be in contact with at least two others. Recording must be carefully carried out and it helps if the child sets out results in tabular form.

Teacher help and information
Adding consecutive numbers produces the triangular numbers – thus:

1	1
1 + 2	3
1 + 2 + 3	6
1 + 2 + 3 + 4	10
1 + 2 + 3 + 4 + 5	15
1 + 2 + 3 + 4 + 5 + 6	21 and so on.

Summing consecutive pairs of triangular numbers gives square numbers.

1	$1 = 1^2$
1 + 3	$4 = 2^2$
3 + 6	$9 = 3^2$
6 + 10	$16 = 4^2$ and so on.

Connections and extensions
The addition of consecutive numbers is also worth exploring. An interesting way of adding consecutive numbers is:

1	2	3	4	5	Using 1–5 inclusive and reversing them gives the same total when summed.
5	4	3	2	1	
6	6	6	6	6	

There are 5 lots of 6 which sums to 30
But we added up two rows so $\frac{30}{2}$ gives 15 which is the sum of 1–5 inclusive.

Link the work on triangular numbers to Investigation 34: Square Numbers.

AT 2 — C34: Square Numbers

Purpose
To explore number patterns.

Resources
Cubes, squared paper (General Copymaster c is 1 cm square.

The task in action
The child should make larger and larger squares and record both the total of the starting unit squares and the number added to make the next largest square. Recording must be done carefully and the children should be encouraged to do this in tabular form.

Teacher help and information
The patterns that the children should develop are:

Number of Square	Size of Square	Unit Total	Squares Added
1	1 (1^2)	1	
2	2 × 2 (2^2)	4	3
3	3 × 3 (3^2)	9	5
4	4 × 4 (4^2)	16	7
5	5 × 5 (5^2)	25	9

Summing a series of odd numbers starting with 1 always results in a square number:

1	1 = 1^2
1 + 3	4 = 2^2
1 + 3 + 5	9 = 3^2
1 + 3 + 5 + 7	16 = 4^2
1 + 3 + 5 + 7 + 9	25 = 5^2 and so on.

Connections and extensions
Link this work with Investigation 33: Triangular numbers.

AT 2 — C35: Palindromes

Purpose
To explore numbers which are characterised by their being identically written whether read from left or right.

Resources
Reference books including a set of history reference books, calculators.

The task in action
The child should try out computations which lead to answers which are 'palindromes'. Having done this they should be able to make some general statements about the sorts of rules that need to be followed to generate such numbers. Calculators may be useful as they offer quick feedback on the trials. The child should also look for palindromic dates and find out what events took place at those times.

Teacher help and information
A palindrome is a word or sentence which reads the same whether read from the left or the right. The term has been borrowed and applied to numbers. There are a variety of ways that palindromic numbers can be generated besides the multiplication example on the Copymaster. One is to start with a number, reverse its digits and add the two together:

12 + 21 = 33
15 + 51 = 66
24 + 42 = also 66

but, not all numbers will do this readily. There are numbers which would need a number of additions, for example:

28 + 82 = 110

but if you then:

110 + 011 = 121 you do get a palindrome.

Some numbers take many more addition steps and some may have no palindromic solution.

Connections and extensions
This investigation can be extended in a variety of ways:
• let the child look for palindromic words and sentences. Common examples include:
MADAM I'M ADAM
ABLE WAS I 'ERE I SAW ELBA (Associated with Napoleon)
A MAN, A PLAN, A CANAL – PANAMA!
• explore the symmetrical ideas that palindromes can generate
• create a future time when the year is palindromic and society values symmetrical objects, music and poetry above all other things. Design some artifacts and write some music and poetry.

Other Investigations that could be used in relation to this one are Investigation 72: Music by Chance (see Connections and extensions). See also Investigation 40: Symmetry: Badges, and Investigation 53: Symmetry: Letters and Numerals.

C36: Best Buy

Purpose
To explore the idea of 'best buy' including the effects of price reductions, percentage price cuts and 'bulk buy' offers.

Resources
Paper or card, old catalogues or magazines, glue, scissors.

The task in action
The children, working in pairs or small groups, should create their own shops using pictures of items they can sell from old magazines, or pictures they have drawn themselves. They can assemble these on a cardboard shop window and add some of the price tags from the Copymaster or make some of their own. Using the goods in their own and others' shops, they can calculate the prices of 'shopping lists' of items.

Teacher help and information
Set the children some challenges, including, for example, some of the following:

- reduce prices by 20% and create and total a new shopping list
- if profits are usually 7.5% and there is an offer of 5% off everything during 'happy hour', how will this affect profits during that time?

Connections and extensions
After some practice the children can set each other problems. Keep the shop windows the children made and the challenges they enjoyed to use with another set of children.
See also Investigation 48: Drinks Survey.

C37: Think of a Number

Purpose
To use number games involving a variety of computations to produce puzzles.

Resources
Calculators may be useful after the children have tested their ideas out using mental arithmetic.

The task in action
The child should work through the example given on the Copymaster and then try to explain how it works. Using the rules they have identified they should then produce examples of their own, which they can try out on their friends.

Teacher help and information
This sort of number game is set up by the challenger and it is in the development of the challenge that the investigation work happens. So, whilst it is fun to try out your efforts on others it is the generation of the problems that is essential. The child will get lots of opportunities to both practise their own computational skill and see the effects of different combinations of computational operations. All the puzzles would prove a useful classroom resource.

Connections and extensions
Connect with Investigation 46, 47: Function Machines.

C38: Story of 2

Purpose
To carry out an exhaustive investigation into the uses of a number; in this case, the number 2.

Resources
These could include a '2 resource box' with pictures, postcards, story titles, examples of pairs, notation of two in a variety of cultures and other examples in it.

The task in action
The child should make a list of all of the 2 related facts that they can. They should use their own knowledge but also question others about the number 2, and look around them, look at pictures and in books.

Teacher help and information
Try to help the children to think imaginatively about the task. If they plan the work as a group they may decide that each child looks at one aspect of 2. Take the cue from what the children want to record. Here are some suggestions if ideas are short:

- famous pairs (twins, Tom and Jerry, etc)
- two in story and rhyme
- left and right
- mirror symmetry
- notation in a variety of cultures
- games with two players, two balls, etc.

Connections and extensions
See also Investigation 40: Symmetry: Badges, Investigation 50: Finding out about Numbers, and Investigation 53: Symmetry: Letters and Numerals.

AT 4 | C39: Questionnaire ▷

Purpose
To investigate the construction and use of questionnaires as tools for gathering data.

Resources
Photocopying or other reproduction facilities, computer with word-processing/ publishing software.

The task in action
The child, or children in pairs, have to use the suggestions offered on the Copymaster to either write out or invent their own questionnaire. They then use it to get replies from a sample of ten people and, on the basis of this experience, suggest improvements to the questionnaire. Using this information the children should then produce a new questionnaire which can be used with a different sample of children. They are finally asked to record the most important things they have learned as 'rules' for questionnaire writers.

Teacher help and information
There are many important concepts to learn in exploring research methods. Try focusing on one or two key ideas and leave others for the next time the children are using questionnaires. Here are some important issues about questionnaires, for the children to be introduced to:

- What's the problem? Choosing what it is you want to find out and making it manageable.
- What to ask? Trying to avoid bias or ambiguity in questions.
- Sampling; volunteers, just boys, or only nine year olds is a biased sample. Does that matter?
- Piloting is an important aspect of questionnaire design and the children should become accustomed to the refinement of their work.
- Recording the answers; is the questionnaire administered face to face or filled in by the respondent on their own?

Note that the size of sample for the second questionnaire in this Investigation is not set. Discuss with the children the constraints on their size of sample, and what this does to the validity of the results.

Connections and extensions
Make a collection of reports from newspapers which give the results of questionnaire surveys. These can be discussed in terms of the size of sample, the interpretation placed and the way in which the survey was carried out.

See also Investigation 41: Survey: Left and Right.

AT 3 | C40: Symmetry: Badges ▷

Purpose
To design a badge or logo using ideas of reflectional and/or rotational symmetry.

Resources
Examples of badges, flags, emblems and logos.

The task in action
The child should look at and analyse a wide variety of badges, emblems, flags and other things which have symmetrical designs. From this they should develop their own ideas about a symmetrical design for a badge, emblem or logo.

Teacher help and information
Discuss with the children, the idea that badges and emblems including national flags, company logos, society badges, and family coats-of-arms convey 'messages'. Talk about the role of these designs in showing, for example, membership of a group, or an image to effect sales.

Connections and extensions
Link this work to Investigation 35: Palindromes, Investigation 53: Symmetry: Letters and Numerals, and Investigation 54, 55: Tiles.

AT 2, 3, 4 | C41: Survey: Left and Right ▷

Purpose
To collect data about left- and right-handedness and footedness and to work out some fractions and percentages using the findings.

Resources
Clipboards.

The task in action
The child needs to interview 20 people, children and/or adults and to complete the table on the Copymaster. Using this data they can work out the fraction and percentages required.

Teacher help and information
If the 20 people interviewed are all right-handed and footed the survey will have to be extended. This is a good opportunity to discuss the idea of 'representative sample' with the children. If a number of children are engaged in this investigation and they all interview different people, the pooling of their results will make the chances of having some left-handers more likely. Comparisons can also be made between one set of 20 results and the results from the entire sample.

Approximately 1 in 10 boys and slightly fewer girls are left-handed.

Connections and extensions
Left-handers are sometimes at a disadvantage. The children may wish to explore all the tools made with the left-handed in mind, and games that can or cannot be played left-handed.
See also Investigation 39: Questionnaire.

C42: Shapes in Buildings: Making a Trail
AT 3

Purpose
To explore the local built environment looking for and identifying 2D and 3D shapes.

Resources
Clipboards.

The task in action
Under supervision the children walk around the locality and identify and make a record of shapes that they see.

Teacher help and information
Have a good look round the neighbourhood without the children first. Then you can plan a route which fits the time you can allow and enables the children to see a range of shapes.

You may need to remind the children of some of the 2D and 3D shapes before your excursion, bearing in mind that it is not always easy, without practice, to identify shapes and spaces in complex structures.

Connections and extensions
Use photography to develop the information about the trail. The trail can then be part of whole school resources and embellished by subsequent groups of children. The trail could form an invaluable addition to resources about the locality, and contribute to study in other areas of the curriculum.

All the Investigations on Shape will support this work.

C43: Prime Numbers
AT 2

Purpose
To identify the Prime Numbers up to 100 and to explore some uses and characteristics of Primes.

Resources
Coloured pencils.

The task in action
Using the Copymaster, the child has to identify the Prime Numbers in a 100 square by means of multiples. To make the task easier let the children use different coloured pencils to shade out numbers which are multiples of smaller numbers.

Teacher help and information
Prime numbers are special and important numbers in mathematics. These are numbers which can only be divided by themselves and one. They have particular importance in the use of factors and factorisation. The children are invited to explore prime factors on the Copymaster but you will need to discuss their findings with them and make use of these in subsequent computational work.

Connections and extensions
Mathematicians still work on Prime numbers and there are many theories about them which are still unproven. Let the children look at the pattern of Primes. For example:

- How far apart are they?
- Where they appear in pairs (with one number between them) is there any particular feature to be observed?
- Can we make addition patterns in Prime numbers? For example:

2 + 7 + 47 = 56
29 + 17 + 3 + 7 = 56

Let the children draw up factor trees for some numbers. Here are two examples:

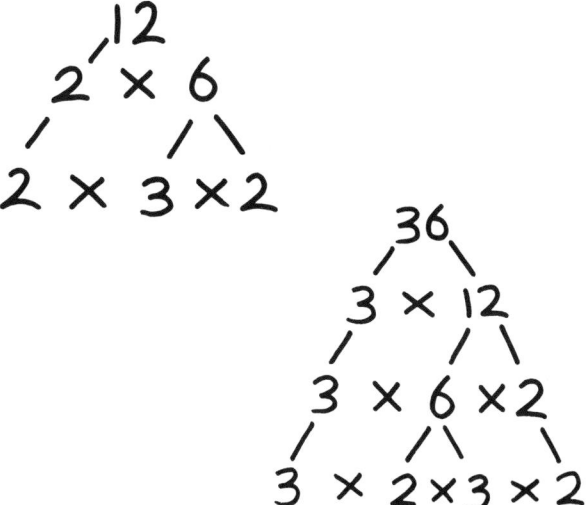

Note that patterns of Primes are not consistent and predictions are actually impossible to make for large numbers.

Link this work to all Investigations related to 'special' numbers, and number series and patterns.

C44, C45: Mazes
AT 3

Purpose
To use a set of tiles to create mazes.

Resources
Card for making tiles more robust if the children wish to re-use them, reference books which give pictures of real mazes.

The task in action
The children are asked to cut out the maze tiles from Copymaster 44 and invent a maze. They can stick the maze down onto Copymaster 45 to make it permanent. They can go on to make a replica of a real maze, using another set of the tiles given on Copymaster 44 or a set of tiles of their own invention, which they can draw in on Copymaster 45.

Teacher help and information
The tiles given will enable children to make mazes that employ right angles. If they then choose to replicate a real maze which is unicursal (see below) or has angles other than right angles they will need to make a new set of tiles with the appropriate shapes on them.

Mazes are very ancient in origin. The word 'Troy' is often associated with the sites of mazes (for example, the Troy Town Maze on St Agnes, Isles of Scilly, Trojeborg maze on Gotland in Sweden) perhaps because the ancient city of Troy was like a maze, a closed city.

Mazes with one pathway to the centre are called 'unicursal'. They can be constructed like this:

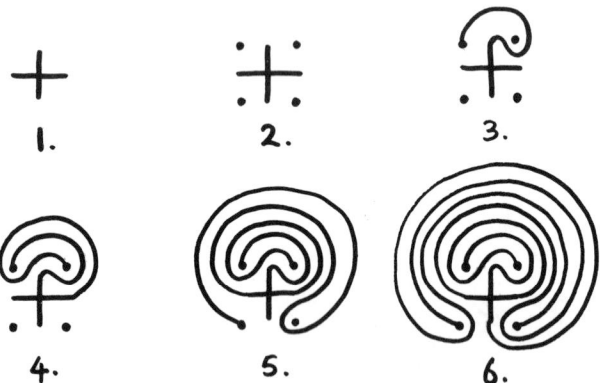

From Fisher, A. and Geister, G., *The Art of the Maze*, Weidenfeld and Nicholson, 1990.

Connections and extensions
Draw a unicursal maze on the playground using chalk.

Numbers of games and books are now available which use the idea of a maze – these are often of the 'Dungeons and Dragons' type although there are some which are based upon, for example, Enid Blyton stories. Some of the children may have games and books which they would like to share with you in a discussion of mazes. There are also numbers of computer games and challenges which have maze-like qualities and are worth exploration!

See also Investigation 25: Town Map, and Investigation 68, 69: Networks.

AT 2 C46, C47: Function Machines

Purpose
To use Function Machines as a means to explore mathematical operations.

Resources
Calculators to check outcomes, after mental arithmetic has been done.

The task in action
On Copymaster 46 the child should work out the output and input numbers for the example machines and then work through a trail where the operations for each machine are clearly defined. Then more trails can be invented.

On Copymaster 46 the child has to try and work out alternative possible operations for the function machines.

Teacher help and information
Copymaster 47 gives children a real experience of a situation in which there is no 'one right answer'. Encourage the children to generate as many possible answers as they can. Write up and display some of them.

Connections and extensions
Invite the children to invent a game which has a series of function machines as challenges, or a wizard who sets 'what happens to the number?' puzzles when players land on magic squares.

See also Investigation 37: Think of a Number.

AT 4 C48: Drinks Survey

Purpose
To investigate the relative costs of different soft drinks and to conduct a survey of children's preferences.

Resources
Carton of orange juice, 4–6 oranges, squeezer, knife, orange squash, water, disposable cups.

The task in action
The three different forms of orange drinks need to be prepared and then 10 children are asked to try each of the three and rate them on taste. The children conducting the investigation need to work out the taste rating and costs for each type of drink.

Teacher help and information
A number of mathematical opportunities are offered in this investigation. The children will have to handle data collection and analysis, and undertake a costing exercise which will involve them in the use of volume and the computation of relative costs.

Connections and extensions
The children could extend their work into a consideration of how to compare the prices of similar products which are prepared or packaged in different ways.

See also Investigation 36: Best Buy.

C49: Polybius Checkerboard Code

AT 2

Purpose
To explore some encoding and decoding systems.

Resources
Paper and a stapler to make a booklet.

The task in action
The child has to use the Polybius Checkerboard, which appears on the Copymaster, to write secret messages and offer them to their classmates. A secret messages booklet can be made and used by pairs of children.

Teacher help and information
The Polybius Checkerboard is an Ancient Greek system. It is important that the child be encouraged to explore the characteristics of the Polybius Checkerboard. In order to put the letters of the alphabet into a 5 × 5 array the letters 'u' and 'v' occupy the same cell. Why these two letters? In order to be able to memorize a coding system it is important that it has a logic which can be memorized and then used to recall the system. In inventing their own secret codes the children should adopt logical strategies and make use of patterning approaches.

Connections and extensions
The Caesar Cipher (named after Julius) goes like this:

a b c d e f g h i j k l m n o p q r s t u v w x y z
d e f g h i j k l m n o p q r s t u v w x y z a b c

This, and other codes that the child can discover, can be used to extend the idea of pattern and logic.
    See also Investigation 4: Codes.

C50: Finding out About Numbers

AT 2

Purpose
To use a wide variety of stimuli to explore a given number.

Resources
Reference books, poetry, music, and nursery rhyme books which contain references to numbers.

The task in action
The child has to choose one of the numbers 3, 5, 7, or 13 and then find out as much as they can about the number in relation to its appearance in sayings, stories, rhymes, superstitions and so on. They must record their findings in the form of a report or poem to be read to or by other children.

Teacher help and information
We have chosen these numbers because they are common in literature and folklore as well as in children's rhymes and playground games. We do not wish to promote magical ideas about numbers but we do see this Investigation as an opportunity for children to come to see numbers as being amenable to their use rather than as symbols removed from real life.

Connections and extensions
Link this work to other parts of the curriculum, and to Investigation 38: Story of 2.

C51: Calendar Month

AT 2

Purpose
To use the layout of dates on a calendar month to look for and explore number patterns.

Resources
Old calendars or diaries with monthly calendar dates.

The task in action
The child can choose any month that they wish and lay out the dates in that month on the Copymaster. They then have to explore the pattern of numbers in the dates, using squares of four and nine adjacent numbers.

Teacher help and information
Exploring number patterns is an excellent way of children mastering three important mathematical skills. They are:

- using computation
- detecting patterns
- making generalisations.

Connections and extensions
The children could be encouraged to go on to explore larger number arrays to see if their generalisations hold for numbers larger than 31 and to see whether they can develop new pattern ideas.
    They could use the stimulus of working with calendars to find out more about dates. For example: leap years, the Gregorian calendar and the work of ancient mathematicians into the periods of the year, and the origins of the names of the days and the months.
    See also Investigation 57: Addition Squares, and Investigation 59: Magic Square.

C52: Tangrams

Purpose
To support the development of ideas to do with area and 2D shapes.

Resources
Scissors.

The task in action
Using the Copymaster the child should cut out the tangram. Using the pieces they should attempt to make a given rectangle and parallelogram as well as pictures of their own design.

Teacher help and information
Tangrams are ancient in origin and different versions of them are available. They offer opportunities for children to be helped to consider the idea of area, for whatever picture or named shape is produced, the area covered by the pieces is always the same. The fact that different regular shapes can be created is important in the children's understanding of transformation, and of the relationships between the different shapes.

Connections and extensions
Try other patterns for tangrams as well as inviting the children to see if they can return the shapes to their original square.
See also Investigation 78: Perimeter and Area.

C53: Symmetry: Letters and Numerals

Purpose
To use letters of the alphabet and numerals to explore ideas to do with reflective and rotational symmetry.

Resources
Plastic mirrors, rough paper.

The task in action
Using the Copymaster the child has to identify letters of the alphabet which display symmetry and go on to find any numerals that are symmetrical.

Teacher help and information
Use the upper-case form of the letters in all cases. Some letters and numerals exhibit both reflective and rotational symmetry whilst others either have one or neither of these characteristics.

A B C D E F G H I
J K L M N O P Q
R S T U V W X
Y Z

O 1 2 3 4 5 6
7 8 9

Connections and extensions
Try using letters from other languages including those from ancient civilizations. This could also be extended to numerals, for example, roman numerals.
  Link to Investigation 40: Symmetry: Badges, and Investigations 54, 55: Tiles.

C54, C55: Tiles

Purpose
To replicate a simple tile to produce patterns showing line and/or rotational symmetry.

Resources
Felt-tips, coloured pencils and wax crayons; 4 cm or 1 inch squared paper (there are one inch squares on General Copymaster b); plastic mirrors.

The task in action
Copymaster 54 invites the child to choose a tile pattern from Copymaster 55, or, using those as inspiration, invent their own. On squared paper they can then replicate their tile to make a variety of patterns, including those showing line and/or rotational symmetry.

Teacher help and information
Supply the children with plastic mirrors to confirm the lines of symmetry.

Connections and extensions
The outcomes of the children's work can make stunning displays, book covers, decorated stationery and designs that can be printed on fabric.

Let the children explore the use of patterns like these in other eras (for example, Victorian decorative tiles) and in other cultures (for example, Rangoli patterns).

See also Investigation 22, 23: Tessellation: Mosaic, Investigation 40: Symmetry: Badges, Investigation 53: Symmetry: Letters and Numerals, and Investigation 76: Tessellation: Pictures.

C56: 9 × Table and Dividing by 9
AT 2

Purpose
To investigate the number patterns in the 9 × table and to learn a quick way to find remainders when dividing by 9.

Resources
Calculator to check computation.

The task in action
The child is asked to write out the 9 × table on the Copymaster and note the patterns in the products, and in the array. A number puzzle is then presented involving division by 9.

Teacher help and information
It is helpful if children can commit tables to memory and 9 × is easier once they know the pattern. The clue to the puzzle solution is that division is repeated subtraction in disguise! Thus, for example:

121 divided by 9 is 13; $(121 - 9) - 9$ and so on to 13 9s, with 4 remainder. 121's reduced number is 4 $(1 + 2 + 1)$ – the remainder!

Connections and extensions
See also Investigation 71: Multiplication Squares and Patterns, and Investigation 65, 66, 67: Pascal's Triangle.

C57: Addition Squares
AT 2

Purpose
To look for addition patterns in 2 by 2 squares.

Resources
Counting aids if necessary.

The task in action
The child has to explore possible patterns in the first two squares on the Copymaster, complete the remaining squares and invent and explore some more.

Teacher help and information
Encourage the children to try 'playing' with the numbers in the squares, and experiment beyond the obvious. For example the children could look at some of the following:

- diagonals
- totals of rows
- totals of columns
- bottom left and top right digits.

Connections and extensions
See also Investigation 51: Calendar Month, Investigation 59: Magic Squares and Investigation 71: Multiplication Squares and Patterns.

C58: Calculator Challenge
AT 2

Purpose
To 'play' with numbers using a calculator.

Resources
A calculator per child!

The task in action
Using a simple letter number code presented on the Copymaster the child is asked to use words to create numbers which can be used in calculations, to give a fixed product or sum.

Teacher help and information
Give the children time to work these games through to their own satisfaction, and, if they enjoy them invite them to set each other challenges.

Connections and extensions
Find and play calculator games.
Link to all number investigations.

C59: Magic Square
AT 2

Purpose
To explore the number patterns present in a special 3 by 3 square, and to look also at patterns in larger squares.

Resources
Calculators to check computations after they have been done.

The task in action
Using the Copymaster the child has to experiment with the number patterns found in a magic square, and create and explore other magic squares.

Teacher help and information
'Magic squares' are so called because of the number patterns in them. The sums of the rows, columns and diagonals are all equal. The earliest known is the Chinese Lo-shu, dating from about 2200 BC. The magic square at the top of Copymaster is a modern equivalent of the Lo-shu. Note that it contains the natural numbers starting from 1, with the 'mid-number' 5 in the centre. The square the child is invited to complete is made up by adding 5 to each of the numbers in the Lo-shu. Fourth and fifth order squares are harder to work through, even numbers (4 × 4) being harder than odds. As well as adding rows, columns and diagonals let the childen look at the sums of the squares of some of the numbers.

Connections and extensions
Link this work to that in Investigation 57: Addition squares, and Investigation 74: Euler's Relation.

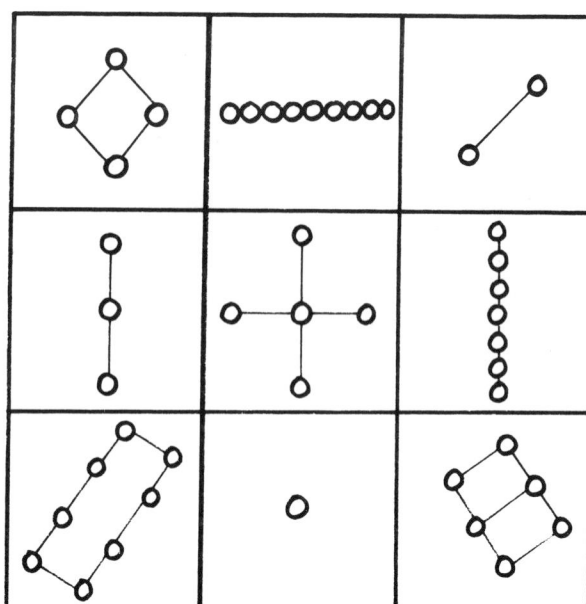

The Lo-shu Magic Square.

Section 3: Level 5

C60: Pentagrams
AT 3

Purpose
To explore the star shape which is known as the Pentagram and to relate some of its characteristics to other patterns in maths.

Resources
Compasses, protractors and set squares.

The task in action
The child has to measure parts of the pentagram on the Copymaster and look at the ratios between measurements and go on to draw their own pentagram of a different size with a view to making measurements and comparisons.

Teacher help and information
Pentagrams were known to and valued by Pythagoras. The pentagon at the centre of the first pentagram can be used to produce another smaller pentagram by drawing lines to connect all of the corners of the central pentagon. It is also the case that joining the outside points of the star with straight lines will produce a larger pentagon which in turn could form the centre of an even larger pentagram.

Connections and extensions
If a number of children undertake this investigation it is useful to tabulate all the ratios they obtain for their different sized pentagrams and find out whether the average of these comes close to the Golden ratio. See also Investigation 68, 69, 70: Fibonacci Series, Golden Ratio and Spirals.

C61: Make a Newsletter
AT 2, 3

Purpose
To use an understanding of scale, plans and shape and size to produce a class newsletter.

Resources
Local newspapers, comics, magazines, A3 or larger sheets of paper scissors, glue, photocopying facilities.

The task in action
The children need to critically examine local newspapers, comics, or children's magazines to establish the essential ingredients of layout and length. They should then use these to extract items which particularly interest them in order to layout their own version of a newsletter.

Teacher help and information
If it is appropriate you can help a group of children to work as a collaborative 'press team' to produce the newsletter, appointing a sports editor, features editor and so on. If the children want to do more than one edition, they can swop jobs, to ensure that both girls and boys get a chance to report on or edit material on a wide variety of issues.

Connections and extensions
If you have access to a desk-top publishing software package the children can go on to design their own paper and fill it with 'copy' they have written themselves.

See also Investigations 68, 69, 70: Fibonacci Series, Golden Ratio and Spirals, for information on paper sizes.

C62: Furniture Design
AT 2, 3

Purpose
To use measurements of children and school furniture as a basis for producing scaled designs of furniture.

Resources
Measuring tapes, metre sticks and rulers, a height chart.

The task in action
The child has to collect data about the dimensions of children's furniture in school and also of a sample of children. From this data they must produce a design or designs for furniture which take account of both function and comfort.

Teacher help and information
Discuss with the children, the issues they need to consider in sampling. They may include:

- age of children
- what constitutes a 'typical' size
- the economic considerations in being able to bulk manufacture to a 'good enough' design.

The child needs to have an understanding of the idea of scale as well as the capacity to carry out reasonably accurate and consistent measuring.

Connections and extensions
Visit the design department of a furniture factory. Let the children look at catalogues of furniture which contain information about dimensions and determine the measurement ranges within which manufacturers are working. Concern for safety could be developed by testing furniture for stability and finding out about fire resistant materials.

Links can be made to Investigation 63: Classroom Planner.

AT 3 | C63: Classroom Planner

Purpose
To give the child the opportunity to work with the idea of scale and the representation of 3D shapes by 2D shapes in plan view.

Resources
Measuring tapes, metre sticks and rulers.

The task in action
The child has to measure the dimensions of the furniture in the classroom and then plan a classroom layout which not only accommodates the necessary furniture but allows for the varied activities that go on in classrooms.

Teacher help and information
Encourage the child to think about scale in relation to the actual dimensions of the classroom and typical furniture. Remind the child that in the scale drawing, everything about the room must be to the same scale, including the contents of the room, width of open doors, space required to push back a chair and stand up and so on.

The child must be clear about the brief. Talk about the kinds of things that need to be taken into account before the child begins. These could include:

- the need for children to be able to move around the room
- the identification of busy spots (e.g. the door) and how the pressure on these might be accommodated
- the nature of different activities which might need different arrangements of furniture
- access to stored items and the storage of children's work, sometimes on a temporary basis (e.g. wet art work).

Connections and extensions
There are many spheres of commercial life in which planning of this type takes place. These include kitchen planning, the building of house extensions, the creation of paths and drives, and the planning of a garden. If possible get some professional planners to share with the children the ways in which they measure and scale their plans.

Let the child design, plan and plant up a miniature garden in a garden trough or large flower pot. Research will be needed to find plants of the right scale to match a doll or clay sculpture or house around which the garden can be built.

Link to Investigation 62: Furniture Design.

AT 2,3 | C64: Vedic Square

Purpose
To explore a way of developing patterns through the use of number combinations.

Resources
Squared paper, coloured pens.

The task in action
Detailed information is given on the Copymaster.

Teacher help and information
The Vedic Square is an ancient Hindu multiplication square which produces symmetrical patterns. Children may need help in finding digital roots i.e. the multiplication $4 \times 3 = 12$ leading to the addition of the 1 and the 2 in 12 to produce the root 3.

In joining together the same numbers it can be quite difficult to see all of them so help the children by suggesting they highlight the numbers with a coloured pen and use another colour to draw in the lines.

Connections and extensions
If you select any of the rows on the Vedic square you can use the sequence of numbers along the row to generate another visual pattern. For example...

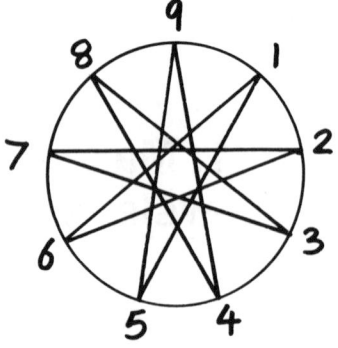

The pattern of numbers in the fifth row of the square
(5 1 6 2 7 3 8 4 9)

Use the tiles generated by the children to make up patterns for floors, materials – try printing some of them using potato cuts, stencils and string print blocks.

Explore other visual patterns from a wide variety of cultures, for example, North American Indian art, Rangoli patterns which are Hindu, Islamic patterns.

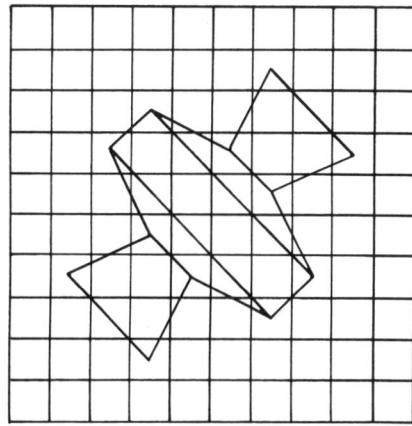

See also Investigation 40: Symmetry: Badges, and Investigation 53: Symmetry: Letters and Numerals.

C65–7: Pascal's Triangle
AT 2, 4

Purpose
To explore Pascal's Triangle for a variety of patterns and develop some ideas to do with probability.

Resources
Possibly collage materials to illustrate the 'spiders on the trellis' problem.

The task in action
On Copymaster 65 the child is presented with Pascal's triangle and invited to look for patterns.

Copymaster 66 presents problems 'spiders on the trellis', and the results of multiples of 11.

On Copymaster 67 the child is invited to work out all the possible outcomes when two, three or more coins are tossed.

Teacher help and information
Blaise Pascal (1623–62) was a talented French mathematician. The patterns presented in Pascal's Triangle include the Fibonacci Series (produced by summing the numbers in the diagonals from top right to lower left). Pascal's Triangle numbers are produced when the 'spiders on the trellis' problem is solved. Remind the child that the 16 or 32 spiders need to go down the panels of trellis until there are groups emerging that would be too small to divide (that is some 'groups' of 1). Multiples of 11 and coin tossing problems also produce Pascal's Triangle numbers. When looking at possible results of coin tossing remind the children that, for example, Head/Tail and Tail/Head are *two* outcomes of throwing two coins. Thus two coins tossed produce a possible outcome pattern that is 1 2 1, and for three coins it is 1 3 3 1.

Connections and extensions
Link the patterns within Pascal's Triangle to Investigation 68, 69, 70: Fibonacci Series, Golden Ratio and Spirals.

C68–70: Fibonacci Series
AT 2, 3

Purpose
To produce a famous number pattern and investigate the ratios between adjacent numbers in the pattern. To explore the use made of the Golden Ratio, and examine how it links to spirals commonly found in the natural world.

Resources
Mathematics resource books, including information about natural spirals. Calculators to check ratios, once they have been worked out. A variety of pieces of paper in some of the standard sizes which are available. Reproductions including details of sizes of some Old Masters, pictures of ancient Greek sculptures.

The task in action
The child is shown, on Copymaster 68, how to make the Fibonacci series by writing two 1s, adding them together and writing that next, and then adding that sum to the number which came before it and writing that next and so on. The child is then asked to compute the ratios between a number of adjacent pairs of numbers in the series.

Copymaster 69 requires the child to investigate the widths and lengths of common paper sizes and some famous paintings to determine which are close to the Golden Ratio. They are also asked to look at reproductions of Greek sculptures of the human figure and determine the ratios between some of the measurements.

Copymaster 70 invites the child to produce a spiral based on squares of Fibonacci Series dimensions, and investigate natural spirals and their links to the same series.

Teacher help and information
Leonardo Fibonacci (1175–c.1250), was an Italian mathematician, who was influential in the introduction of Arabic numerals (on which our current ones are based) into Europe.

The ratios of the pairs of the numbers in the series are all close to 1.62. It is called the Golden Ratio and was very important to the ancient Greeks. They used it to work out the proportions of beautiful buildings like the Parthenon and sculptures and pictures. Some of the measurements that the children make may approximate to this ratio. For example, even on a small scale reproduction of a Greek relief sculpture, they could, using a ruler marked in millimetres, measure the length of the head of one of the figures and the length from chin to navel. It may be that the ratio between these measurements yields a figure close to 1.62. The children can then experiment with other pairs of measurements to see which ratios approach the Golden Ratio.

A spiral drawn using squares of Fibonacci series dimensions, replicates natural spirals found, for example, in shells, horns, the centres of sunflowers and pine cones.

Connections and extensions
Link this work to Investigations 65, 66, 67: Pascal's Triangle.

C71: Multiplication Squares and Patterns
AT 2

Purpose
To reinforce and further explore the effects of multiplying simple numbers together and to further explore the patterns produced in multiplication tables.

Resources
Rulers or 1 cm squared paper (General Copymaster c).

The task in action
The child should complete the squares on the Copymaster and then explore them for patterns. Then the child is invited to look for patterns in multiplication tables.

Teacher help and information
When the numbers used are the same for both the horizontal and vertical components of the array, as is the case with the first example on the Copymaster, the observations that the children might make include:

- column and row totals are symmetrical
- the numbers in the cells of one of the diagonals are square numbers
- the totals of the rows and columns are multiples of the sum of the three numbers involved
- the three numbers in the cells that make the diagonals, when multiplied together, make totals that are equal.

Ask the children to look at whether these kinds of patterns occur in a number of squares.

Connections and extensions
Link this work to Investigation 56: 9 × Table and Dividing by 9, and Investigation 64: Vedic Square.

C72: Music by Chance
AT 4

Purpose
To use musical composition to explore probability and chance.

Resources
Musical instrument, manuscript paper, a die.

The task in action
The children are invited to select three notes that they know, and can play, and use these to develop a tune.

Teacher help and information
If a child gets stuck on the instructions use this as an example to show them what to do: if C, B and G were the chosen notes the six possible combinations are:

CBG, CGB, GCB, GBC, BCG, BGC

If these were to be numbered 1–6 inclusive and a die were rolled eight times (eight is used because eight bar phrases are in common use in composition) a tune will be produced by chance.

Connections and extensions
Try different combinations of notes as some will sound more tuneful than others. Make another pattern by throwing the die four times and using these throws in reverse to produce the eight bars. This produces a 'symmetrical tune' and can be linked to work on reflective symmetry.

See also Investigation 35: Palindromes, Investigation 40: Symmetry: Badges, and Investigation 53: Symmetry: Letters and Numerals.

C73: Angles
AT 2, 3

Purpose
To inspect the interior and exterior angles in a variety of shapes.

Resources
Protractors, a variety of 2D shape templates, including irregular ones.

The task in action
The child is invited to measure the interior angles for a variety of shapes, and also those angles on the exterior which are shown on the Copymaster. They then sum them and try measuring and summing the same angles for shapes which they draw themselves.

Teacher help and information
The general concept that emerges in all the shapes tried is that the summed angles on the exterior match one complete revolution, that is 360°. This is always the case as travelling around any figure once is one complete rotation. The children can gain insights into this through tearing paper:

Internal angles

corners from triangle

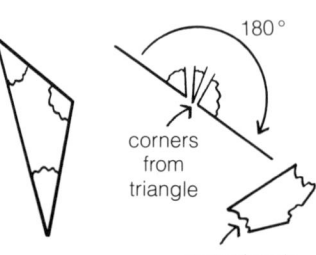
torn triangle

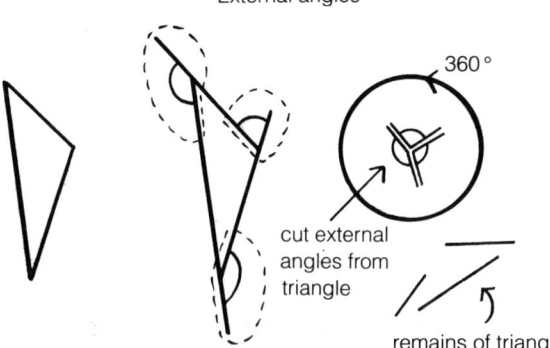

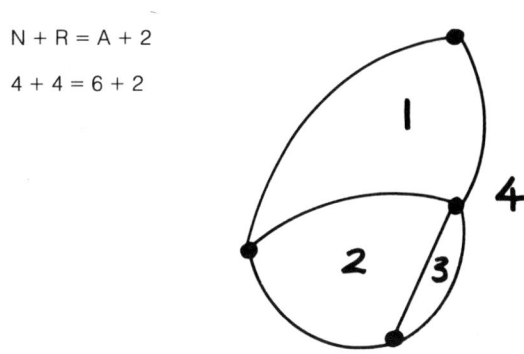

$N + R = A + 2$

$4 + 4 = 6 + 2$

Some children might come to see that a general equation can be established which will give the sum of the interior angles of 2D shapes:

Total of internal angles = Number of vertices (N) × (180 - 360/N)

For regular 2D shapes it is only necessary to divide the Total by the Number of Vertices to establish each interior angle.

Connections and extensions
Link to all the Investigation 76: Tessellation: Pictures.

C74: Euler's Relation
AT 2, 3

Purpose
To look for a relationship between the numbers of faces, vertices and edges in regular 3D shapes.

Resources
A set of mathematically correct 3D shapes.

The task in action
For the shapes listed on the Copymaster the child is asked to list the numbers of faces, vertices and edges, and then try to find a general pattern.

Teacher help and information
Leonhard Euler (1707–83), was a Swiss mathematician, extremely gifted and influential in maths, and physics.

Let the children handle the shapes and physically do the counts required. They will find that, for all these shapes, the following holds:

$F + V = E + 2$ where F = number of faces, V = number of vertices and E = number of edges

Connections and extensions
Ask the children to find out whether the relation holds for shapes which are not regular, that is any polyhedron.

Investigate networks with the children to find out whether the following holds:

$N + R = A + 2$ where N = number of nodes, R = number of regions and A = number of arcs.

See also Investigations 81, 82: Networks.

C75: Handshakes
AT 2, 4

Purpose
To investigate the number pattern involved when a number of people shake hands.

Resources
Triangular Dotty Paper (General Copymaster d).

The task in action
Using any means they like the children are required to produce a table showing how many handshakes occur when everyone in a room shakes hands with everyone else.

Teacher help and information
Encourage the children to be systematic in the way they approach this problem. Triangular dotty paper can help with this. The resultant pattern is that of triangular numbers (that is 0, 1, 3, 6, 10, 15, …).

Connections and extensions
Link this to Investigation 33: Triangular Numbers.

C76: Tessellation: Pictures
AT 3

Purpose
To make shapes that tessellate by translation of part of a regular shape.

Resources
Scissors, rulers, felt-tips or colouring pencils, rough paper, sticky tape.

The task in action
Following the instructions on the Copymaster the child is asked to cut a 'template shape', move part of the shape from one side to the other side of the shape and use this new shape to make tessellating pictures.

Teacher help and information
This task can demand a good deal of manipulative skill. Encourage the children to make the piece they cut out of their shape a simple one.

Connections and extensions
Let the children study the work of M. C. Escher. Tessellations that are more complex than translation can involve rotation. For example a cut piece may be rotated about a corner or the mid-point of a side of a shape.

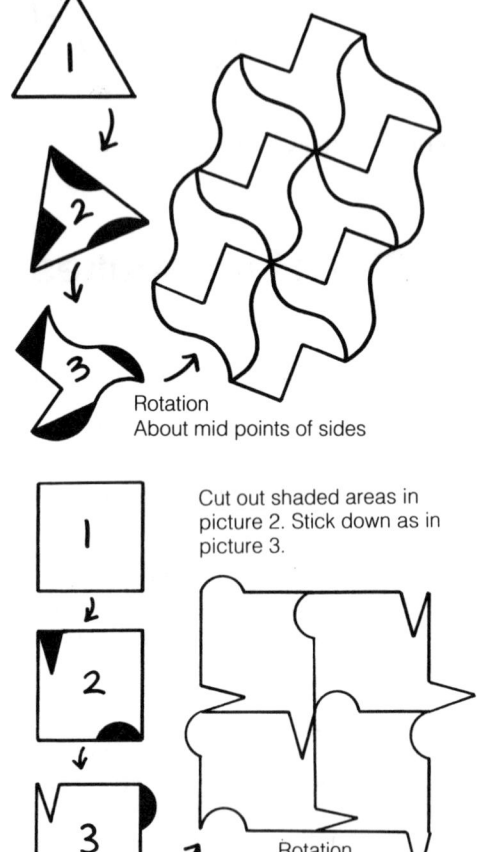

The children could try making some of these.
See also Investigation 73: Angles as well as the earlier Tessellation Investigations.

C77: Napier's Rods
AT 2

Purpose
To make and experiment with a device for doing long multiplication.

Resources
Lolly sticks or strips of card, ruler, rough paper.

The task in action
Using the model on the Copymaster the child is asked to make Napier's Rods. They then choose a number which is to be multiplied and select the rods that correspond to the digits in the number. If these are laid in the appropriate order, side by side, the row for the chosen multiple will provide the answer through the summing of the diagonals in that row. Examples for 258×5 and 258×6 are on the Copymaster.

Teacher help and information
These are named after a Scotsman John Napier, 1550–1617. He invented logarithms.

Connections and extensions
Link this work to other Investigations into multiplication.

C78: Perimeter and Area
AT 2, 3

Purpose
To find out more about perimeter and area.

Resources
Geoboards with rubber bands, squared paper (there are 5 mm squares on General Copymaster A and 1 inch squares on General Copymaster B).

The task in action
Using geoboards or squared paper the child is asked to make some shapes, make a set of shapes having the same number of squares (same area) and inspect their perimeters. The final task is to try making some shapes with the same perimeters but different areas.

Teacher help and information
The children may find it easier to begin with squared paper, and colour the squares within a shape. They can then count the 'sides of squares' around the shape to give a count for perimeter.

Connections and extensions
Link this to Investigation 26: Polyominoes.

C79: The Number 1089
AT 2

Purpose
To use the number 1089 as a means to encourage the investigation of 'special' numbers.

Resources
A calculator to check computations as necessary.

The task in action
Following the instructions on the Copymaster the child can try the puzzle with several three digit numbers. It looks like magic!

Teacher help and information
1089 is fascinating, for as the children will discover, the puzzle always gives the answer 1089 with a reduced number 9. If we look at multiples of 1089:

$$1089 \times 1 = 1089$$
$$\times 2 = 2178$$
$$\times 3 = 3267$$
$$\times 4 = 4356$$
$$\times 5 = 5445$$
$$\times 6 = 6534$$
$$\times 7 = 7623$$
$$\times 8 = 8712$$
$$\times 9 = 9801$$

The columns in the products show a pattern, and all the products have the reduced number 9.

Connections and extensions
Link to all number Investigations. Seek out other 'special' numbers.

C80: Snooker
AT 3

Purpose
To investigate the pathways and number patterns made by balls on an imaginary 'snooker' table.

Resources
Squared paper (there are 5 mm squares on General Copymaster a).

The task in action
The child is asked to work out the routes taken by balls on a number of imaginary snooker tables of different sizes.

Teacher help and information
Remind the children that the angles of incidence and reflection must be equal in their drawings and at 45°. The ball only crosses every square if the numbers of squares along both sides do not have a common factor.

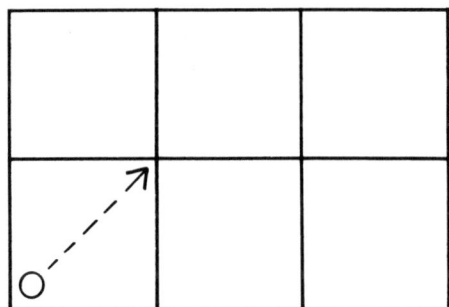

Connections and extensions
Let the children watch some snatches of video of real snooker games. They can freeze the frame and draw the actual route taken by some of the balls.

Link this work to Investigation 84: Celtic Knots.

Section 4: Extension Investigations Beyond Level 5

C81, C82: Networks
AT 3

Purpose
To develop ideas and rules about the traversability of networks.

Resources

The task in action
The child has to see whether the net on Copymaster 81 is traversable. As it is not, the child is invited to suggest ways of making it traversable, and is asked to look at the number of routes meeting at each location in the town. This can provoke the child to suggest some general rules about nets that are traversable, and test these out on the nets on Copymaster 82.

Teacher help and information
For a net to be traversable the child must be able to travel every line on the net once and once only. The net on Copymaster 81 can be made traversable by removing a route from one of the locations at the junction of three routes, or putting in an extra route at one of these locations. In either case the number of locations or 'nodes' with an odd number of routes would be reduced to two. This conforms to the rule that to be traversable, a net must have two but no more than two odd nodes. (A start is made at one odd node and a finish at the other). It would also be traversable if all the nodes were even. (In this case the start can be made anywhere and the finish is at the same place.)

Connections and extensions
Let the children create nets for one another to solve, using, for example, geoboards and thread to create the pathways, or a programmable computer robot to traverse pathways set on the hall floor.
Link this work to Investigation 44, 45: Mazes.

C83: Knots
AT 3

Purpose
To encourage the interpretation, and representation, of 3D shapes and movements in 2D form.

Resources
String or thick wool, reference books containing information about knots – these might include encyclopædias, camping books, Scout and Guide books, and angling books.

The task in action
The children have to attempt to make the knots illustrated on the Copymaster. They have to produce step by step diagrams showing intermediate steps to illustrate exactly how to tie two of the knots. They are invited to find out more about knots and to relate particular knots to situations and occupations.

Teacher help and information
The problems in making 2D representations of 3D objects and movements are highlighted in this activity. Discuss with the children the possible strategies they may adopt to make the diagrams easier to understand. For example, they may decide that the thread to the 'fore' of the picture should be a different colour, that the 'back' thread should be shaded, that computer graphics are essential to produce good diagrams, that there should be conventions about what happens first in a knot (perhaps right over left takes precedence).

Connections and extensions
Link this to Investigation 84: Celtic knots (where a different set of rules are operating).

C84: Celtic Knots
AT 3

Purpose
To investigate the way in which Celtic Knots are constructed and to use this to construct some more.

Resources
Books with knot patterns and various borders e.g. Book of Kells, reproductions of illuminated lettering.

The task in action
The child is asked to replicate a Celtic knot design and study some examples of such knots. A border can then be produced by linking a number of knots together.

Teacher help and information
This investigation is essentially concerned with networks. The knot on the Copymaster can be made using one continuous line. Knots of other dimensions may require more than one line. It is a phenomenon used in quilting.

Connections and extensions
Ask the children to research continuous line puzzles from a variety of cultures. The children could try to replicate Celtic knot designs using an appropriate graphics software package on the computer.

This work can be linked directly to Investigation 80: Snooker.

| AT 3 | **C85: Plaiting** |

Purpose
To explore the sequences involved in plaiting.

Resources
A range of different coloured wools, graph or squared paper, coloured pens or pencils.

The task in action
Using the Copymaster the child starts by plaiting three strands. Having worked through a three strand plait to establish its cycle the child then moves on to exploring further numbers of strands. In order to keep track of the strands the child can draw each row on squared paper using coloured pens or pencils. Here is the three strand plait:

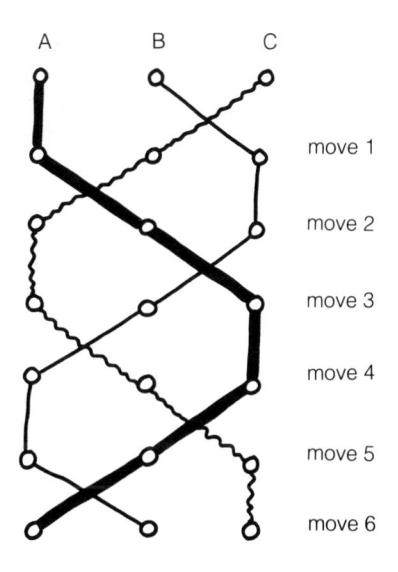

Teacher help and information
Plaiting supports a discussion of sequences. It is closely related to patterns in dance (country and May-pole) and bell-ringing. Bell-ringers, as well as dancers, usually alter the penultimate change so that a return to the start is avoided.

Connections and extensions
There are many everyday experiences which have mathematical bases. These include cross-stitch, knitting and weaving as well as plaiting, dancing and bell-ringing. All are worth exploring.

See also Investigation 83: Knots, and Investigation 84: Celtic Knots.

Whole school investigations

If work is planned across the whole school or department, it is possible to tackle Investigations which take in work at a range of Levels. The work could then be undertaken by, for example, a number of children from a variety of age groups, a number of whole classes or the whole school. The outcomes of work like this can be set out in the following ways:

- a whole school display, taking in space in every classroom
- a 'visitor' display in the 'public' areas of the school like the entrance hall
- an exemplar display for the staff room.

There follow some examples of the kinds of topics that can be treated as 'whole school' and some of the ways of managing outcomes. Copymasters are not provided for these examples, for the recording the children do will depend on a variety of factors including the Levels at which they are working and the kind of activity.

A: Games Bonanza
AT 2, 3, 4

Purpose
To explore a variety of card and board games, and find out the rules of play, and whether the game relies on chance or strategy for a win.

Resources
A wide range of games, from school resources and that the children have brought into school.

The task in action
Invite the children in groups, to choose a game, play it several times and write a report. The report may contain some of the following:

- an analysis of how the game is played
- a list of the rules
- the merits of the game
- the game's weaknesses
- skills necessary to play
- whether the game is fair.

Teacher help and information
You may like to invite several groups of children to play a game, and have the report compiled as a kind of opinion survey. Children at Levels 1 and 2 can try 'Beetle Drive', track games like 'Snakes and Ladders', pattern making, timing, Snap, happy families, and colour matching games. For children at levels 3 and 4 quiz games, draughts, patience and adventure games can all be included. At levels 5 and 6 the children can tackle elaborate maze games, classic card games and chess.

Connections and extensions
On the basis of the children's results they can compile a games resource list for the school, to include all those games the school should buy!

The children can experiment in making some of their own games. There are some ideas about this in Investigations within this book.

Have a 'games day' when all the games are available for anyone to play. Arrange a display of the 'Top 30' games and all the children's reports and invite the parents in to see them, so that they can add the best to Christmas and birthday lists.

B: School Maths Day
AT 2, 3, 4

Purpose
To give the children the chance to work with some really big numbers that they can be reminded of every day in school.

Resources
Access to all parts of the school, and a variety of measuring instruments, including electronic sensors if available.

The task in action
On a planned 'Maths Day' give groups of children and their teachers challenges to do with the whole school. Depending on the kind of building you work in and the resources available, these challenges could include, perhaps, some of the following:

- find the volume of air in the hall
- find the dimensions of the hall
- estimate how many bricks were used to build the school
- how many children have attended the school since it opened
- what are the basic needs for each classroom (chairs, tables, pencils, paper, etc)
- estimate how many steps are taken by each child as they move around school in a day
- what is the temperature difference, or noise difference between the lowest/highest or noisiest/quietest in the school.

Teacher help and information
Children and teachers may be able to generate a list of things they want to discover.

Connections and extensions
Collate all the children's findings into a large book for the library.

AT 3 | C: Doing Time ▷

Purpose
To explore time through a variety of activities.

Resources
Stopwatches and timers.

The task in action
Let the children do a variety of activities related to the concept time. The choice of enquiry will depend on the outcomes of discussion with them and their teachers, but could include the following:

- an investigation into sun dials, what they look like, their history, how they work, how accurate they are
- an assembly of sports records indicating the times taken for various Olympic events
- a time check on the school day for a week, to find out how much time is spent waiting, queueing and doing other things that are not really useful
- timing of the evacuation of the school for a fire practice
- a list for 5, 6, 7, year-olds of some things they can do in a second or a minute; they can invent them but here are some starter suggestions: second: hear their heart beat, jump, say their name twice, bang a drum, blink five times; minute: hop on one leg, run to the door, put their coat on
- inspect all the clocks in school and ask a sample of people which is the easiest to read; list the crucial considerations in clock face design, including the presentation of the numerals.

Teacher help and information
With a little planning among all the teachers comprehensive coverage of what the children need to know about time can be covered in the course of this Investigation.

Connections and extensions
This Investigation could contribute to science, technology and history projects for some classes in the school.

AT 4 | D: Data Day ▷

Purpose
To explore a variety of ways of getting, storing and presenting information.

Resources
The prime sources of first hand information are the children and adults in school; clipboards may also be useful to some of the children.

The task in action
Let each group or class of children decide on some information that they would like to find out from other people in school. Let them discuss with their teachers how they might collect, collate and present that information. Convene a meeting of reporters to feed in the kinds of information each group is assembling. Check there is little overlap between groups, and that a variety of methods are being used. Let the children have free access to each other's classes. Invite them to set out the information they have in an attractive way and display it in the hall at the end of the day.

Teacher help and information
Individual teachers can be on hand to help the groups in their classes. To spur the children's thinking the information can include, for example, facts like family size; attitudes like what the children think of school, and feelings like how do they feel when there is a thunderstorm. Methods of information collection include observation, questionnaires and interviews. The outcomes can be presented as, for example, sets, tallies, block graphs, line graphs.

Connections and extensions
Give all the children a guided tour of everyone's work. Invite some of the children to help create a school data base using all the information. Collate all the information into a 'school report' for everyone to see.

AT 2 | E: Number Puzzles ▷

Purpose
To assemble and work out a collection of number puzzles.

Resources
Children, teachers, parents, governors and other adults known to the school, and a variety of counting aids, construction toys, computers and calculators.

The task in action
Invite everyone to bring or send in to school their own favourite number puzzles, including those that appear in comics and magazines, those that are part of a game, computer games and those that people have invented themselves. Make an exhibition and then invite everyone to come and try them out.

Teacher help and information
Start the collection by using a staff meeting to generate some number puzzles.

Connections and extensions
Consult the school library, public library, maths advisor and local Teacher Education Institution to add more puzzles to the collection. Compile, with the help of the children, books of puzzles for children in different parts of the school.

Name _____

Level 1/2: Shape, space & measures

Measures 1

Draw things you find are good to measure with these:

lolly stick	string	handspan	stride

Copymaster 1

Name _____ Level 1/2: Number/Handling data

Making faces

How many faces can you make?

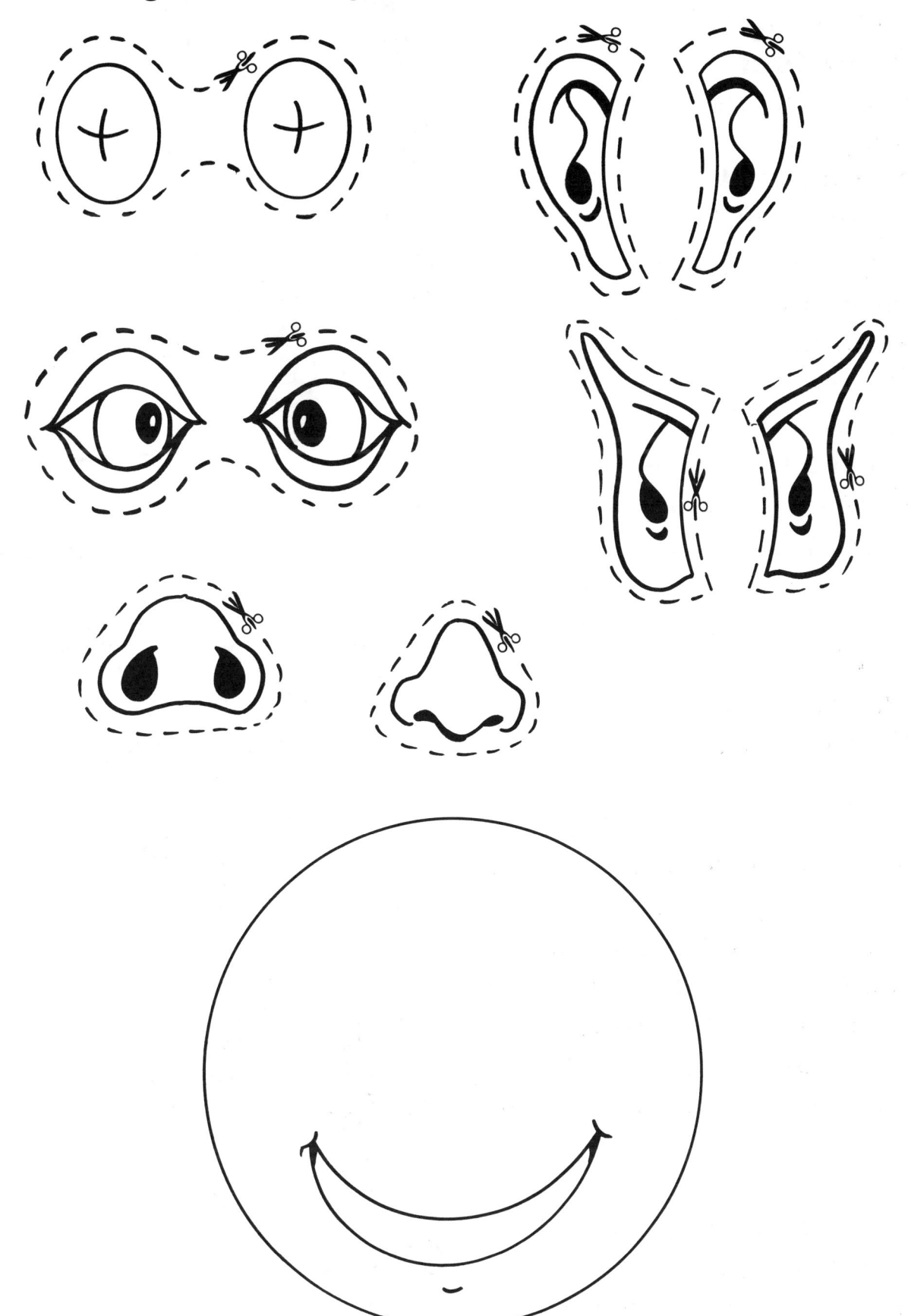

Copymaster 2

Name _____

Level 1/2: Number

Counting songs and rhymes

One, two
Buckle my shoe;
Three, four
Knock at the door;
Five, six,
Pick up sticks;
Seven, eight,
Lay them straight;
Nine, ten,
A big fat hen;
Eleven, twelve,
Dig and delve;
Thirteen, fourteen,
Maids a-courting;
Fifteen, sixteen,
Maids in the kitchen;
Seventeen, eighteen,
Maids in waiting;
Nineteen, twenty,
My plate's empty.

One, two, three, four, five,
Once I caught a fish alive,
Why did you let it go?
Because it bit my finger so.
Six, seven, eight, nine, ten,
Shall we go to fish again?
Not today, some other time,
For I have broke my fishing line.

One, two, three, four,
Mary at the cottage door,
Five, six, seven, eight,
Eating cherries off a plate.

Copymaster 3

Name _____

Level 1/2: Number

Codes

Semaphore

Make this signal first. It shows that numbers not letters follow.

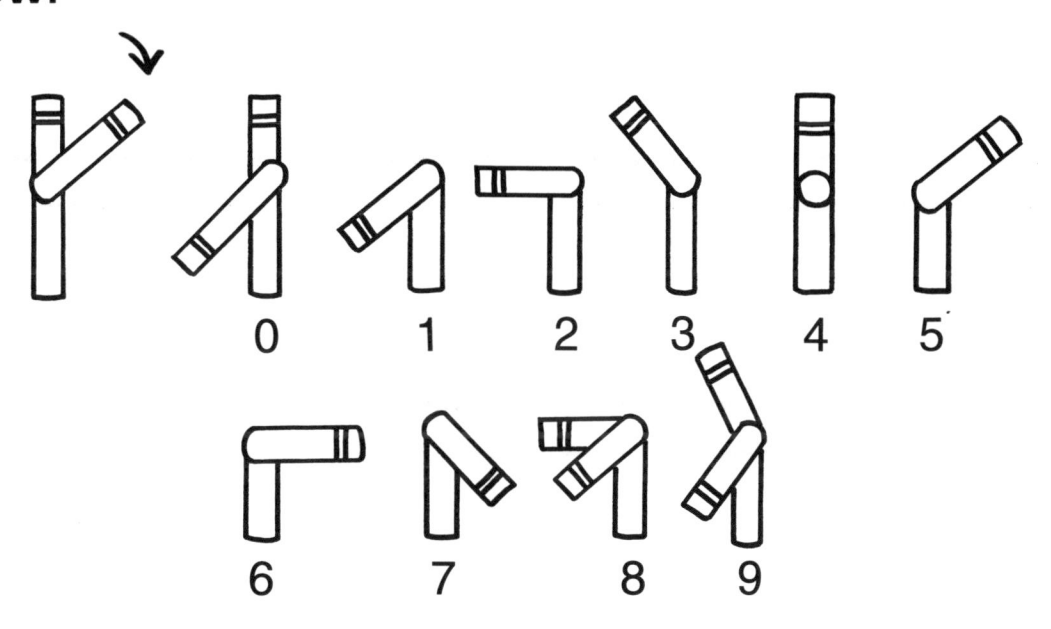

0   1   2   3   4   5

6   7   8   9

Morse

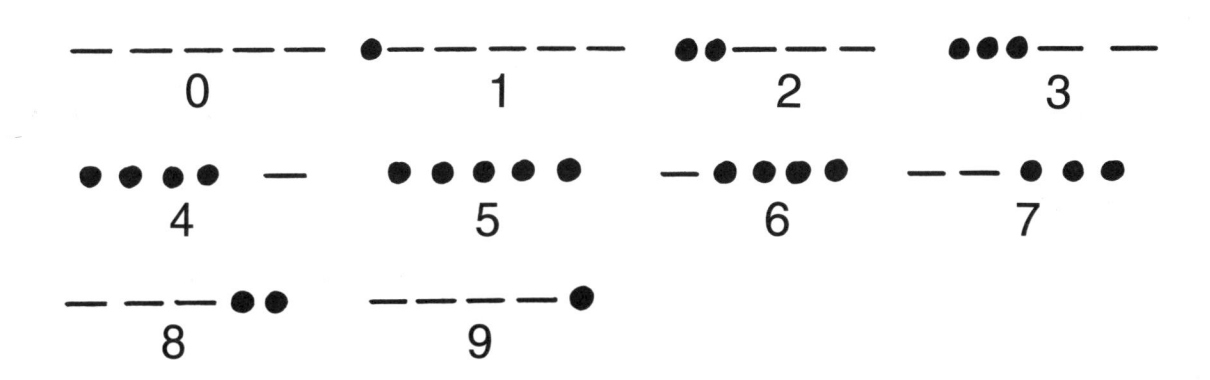

– – – – –   • – – – –   • • – – –   • • • – –
    0   1   2   3

• • • • –   • • • • •   – • • • •   – – • • •
    4   5   6   7

– – – • •   – – – – •
    8   9

Invent your own number code which follows a pattern. Set some number challenges for your classmates.

Copymaster 4

Name _____

Level 1/2: Shape, space & measures

Flick and roller books

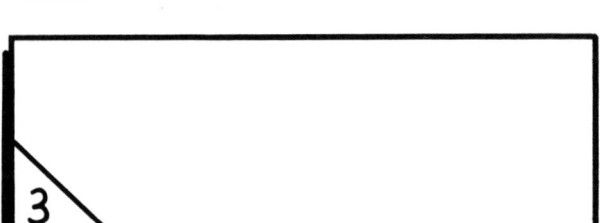

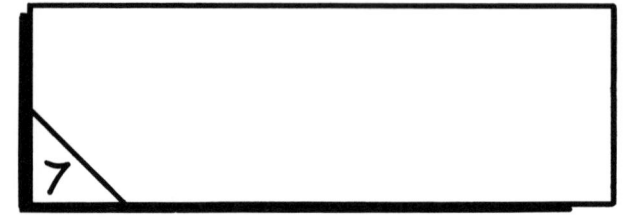

Make a flick book.

1	2
3	4
5	6
7	8

Make a roller book.

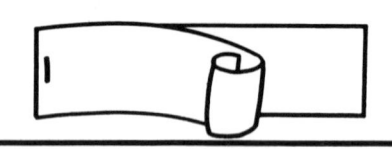

Copymaster 5

Name _____

Level 1/2: Number

Legs

Draw an animal with:

2 legs

4 legs

6 legs

8 legs

What else comes in 2s, 4s, 6s and 8s?

Copymaster 6

Name _____   Level 1/2: Shape, space & measures

3D shapes in the classroom

Find something to match each of these shapes.

Draw it inside the right shape.

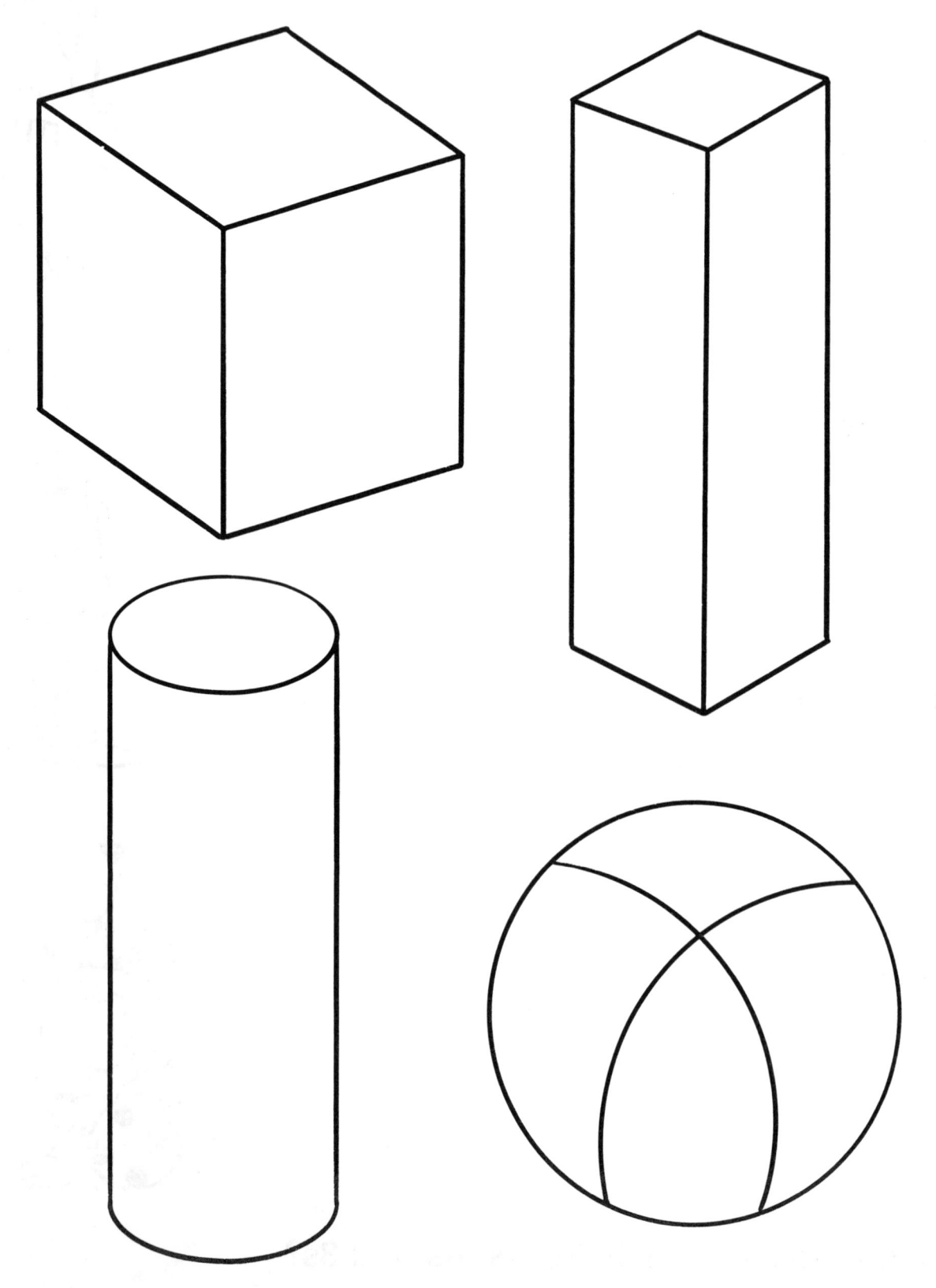

Copymaster 7

Name _____

Level 1/2: Shape, space & measures

2D shapes in the classroom

Find something to match each of these shapes.

Draw it inside the right shape.

Copymaster 8

Name _____ Level 1/2: Number

Bear race

Does each Ted have the same chance?

How many throws in a game?

How few throws?

Is it better to get a 6 or a 1?

Try moving backwards when you throw an odd number.

Invent some new rules.

Start   **Start**

Copymaster 9

Name _____

Level 1/2: Number/Handling data

Bus sorts

Colour the bus

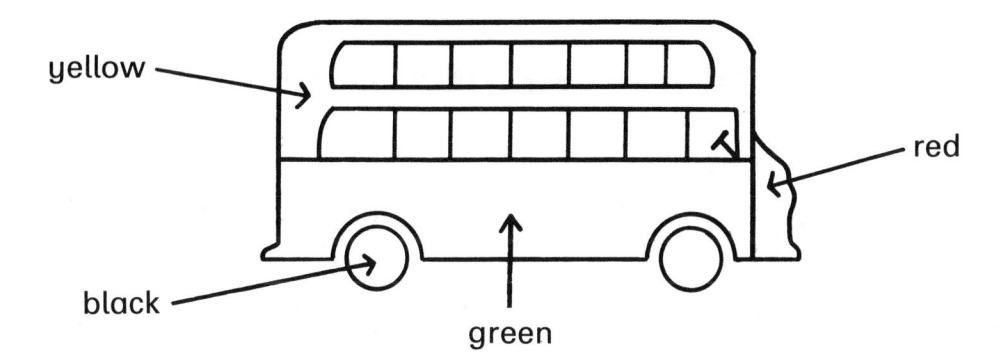

yellow
red
black
green

Use the same colours to make some different buses.

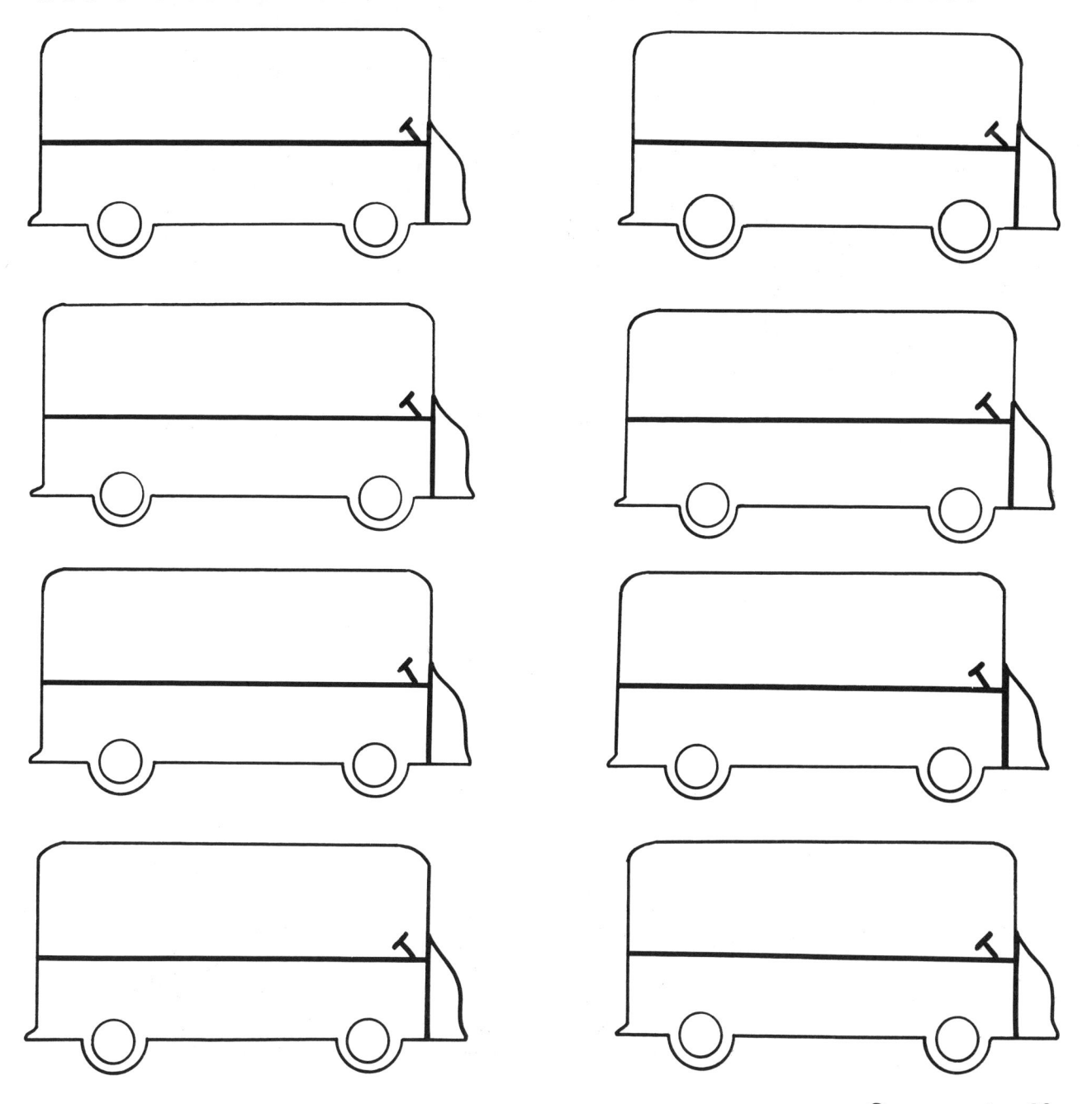

Copymaster 10

Name _____   Level 1/2: Shape, space & measures

Cross stitch

Make a cross stitch picture.

Work out the pattern on squared paper.

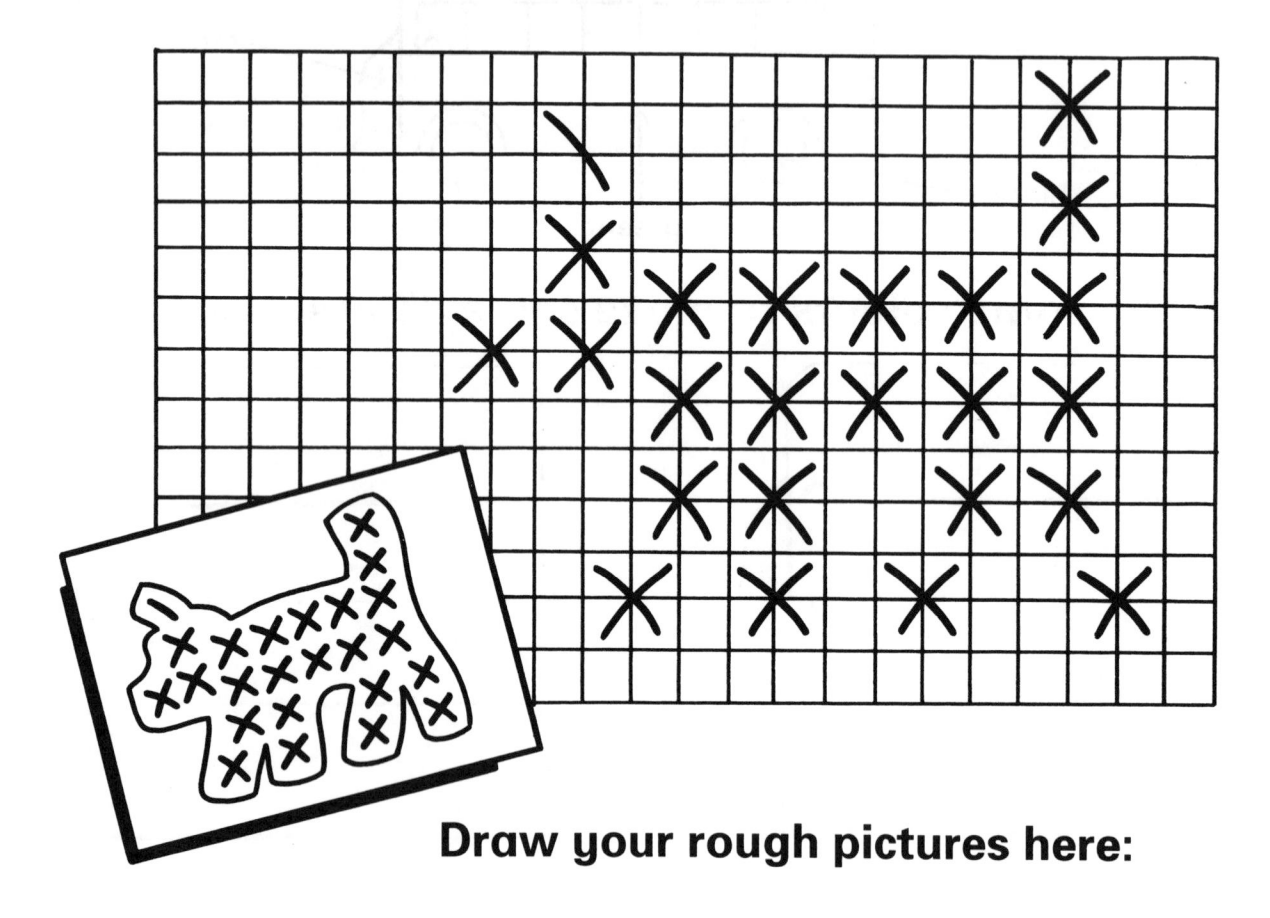

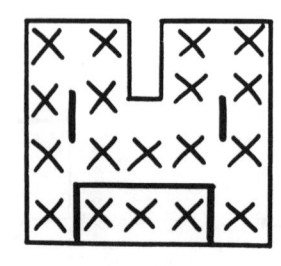

Draw your rough pictures here:

Copymaster 11

Name _____

Level 1/2: Number/Shape, space & measures/Handling data

Game Maker: Game track

Copymaster 12

Game Maker: Game board

Level 1/2: Number/Shape, space & measures/Handling data

51	50	31	30	11	10
52	49	32	29	12	9
53	48	33	28	13	8
54	47	34	27	14	7
55	46	35	26	15	6
56	45	36	25	16	5
57	44	37	24	17	4
58	43	38	23	18	3
59	42	39	22	19	2
60	41	40	21	20	1

Copymaster 13

Name _____   Level 1/2: Number/Shape, space & measures/Handling data

Game Maker: Game pieces (1 of 2)

Jump on 3

Go back 2

Have another go

Go on 5

Have another go

Go on 3

Go back 3

Go on 2

Go on 6

Jump on 4

MISS A GO

Zog!

Wham!

Zzz!

Copymaster 14

Name _____   Level 1/2: Number/Shape, space & measures/Handling data

Game Maker: Game pieces (2 of 2)

Zip! Ping! Zap!

Boof! Bop! Pow!

Copymaster 15

Name _____ Level 1/2: Shape, space & measures

Maze game

Work out a route this way <------> and this way ↕.

Find a really long route.
Cut out the dragons and block some paths.

Copymaster 16

Name _____

Level 1/2: Number

Number play

**Play with these numerals.
Make a really big number.**

Write all the additions you can do with these numerals.

What is the smallest number you can make with two numerals?

Copymaster 17

Name _____

Level 1/2: Number/Handling data

Pocket sort

Sort these in all the ways you can.

Draw in something you sometimes have in your pocket.

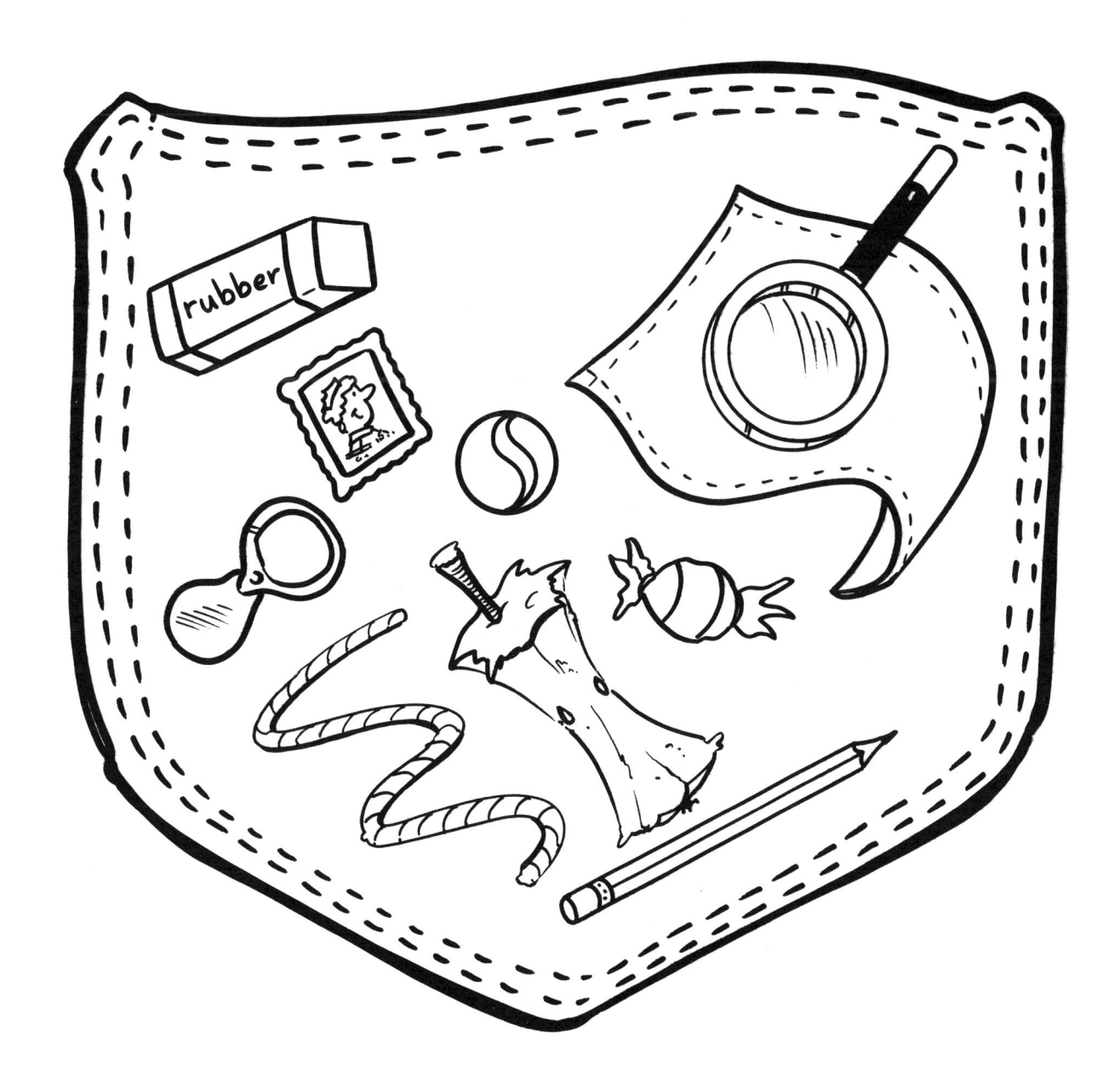

**Now do some more sorts.
Talk about your sorts.**

Copymaster 18

Name _____ Level 1/2: Shape, space & measures

Road signs

Find some road signs.

Draw what you see.

Copymaster 19

Name _____

Level 1/2: Shape, space & measures

Shape check

Use the shapes to check:

Do they pack?

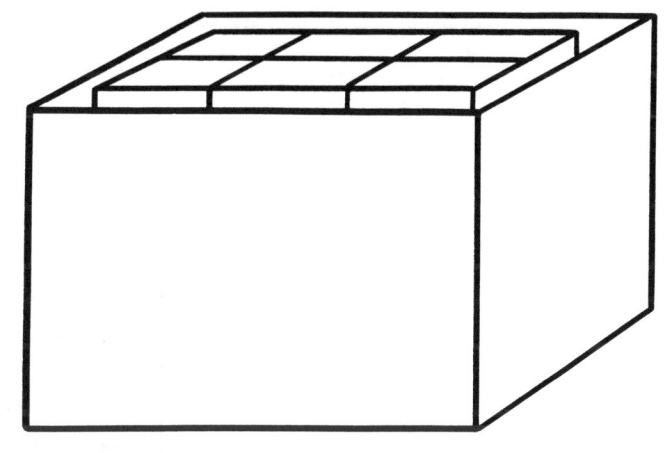

Do they stack?

What do we use them for?

Do they roll?

Copymaster 20

Name _____

Level 1/2: Number/Shape, space & measures

Tessellation: Bricks

Draw patterns of bricks you have seen.

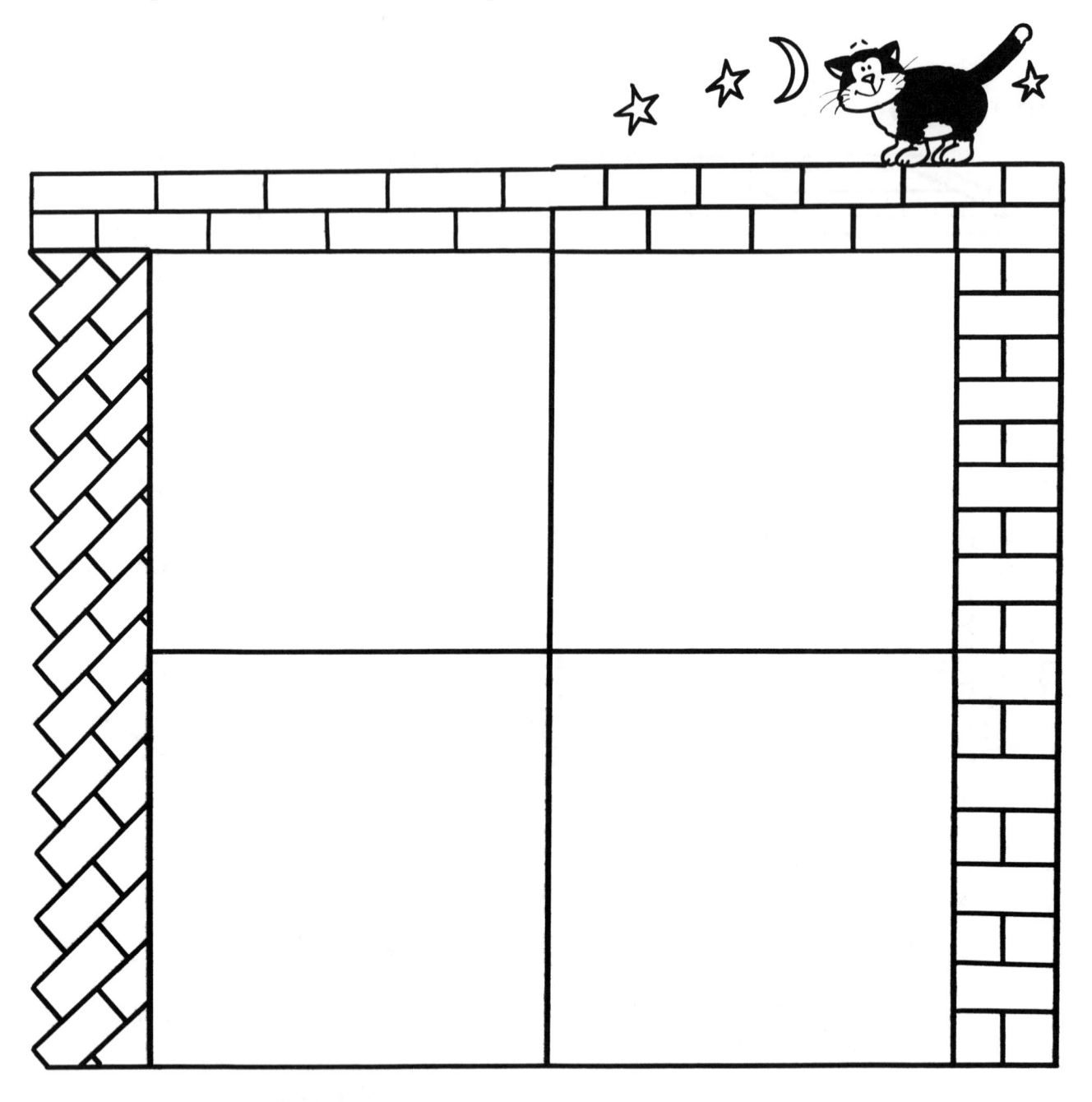

Make up a pattern of bricks.

Copymaster 21

Name _____

Level 1/2: Shape, space & measures

Tessellation: Mosaic (1 of 2)

Copymaster 22

Name _____

Level 1/2: Shape, space & measures

Tessellation: Mosaic (2 of 2)

Tick shapes that fit together with no spaces.

□

⬠

⬢

△

□ and △

⯃ and □

Copymaster 23

Name _____   Level 1/2: Number

Traffic lights

Colour in the sequence.

Traffic lights.

Traffic lights at a Pelican crossing.

For cars

For people using the crossing

Copymaster 24

Name _____

Level 3/4: Number/Shape, space & measures

Town map

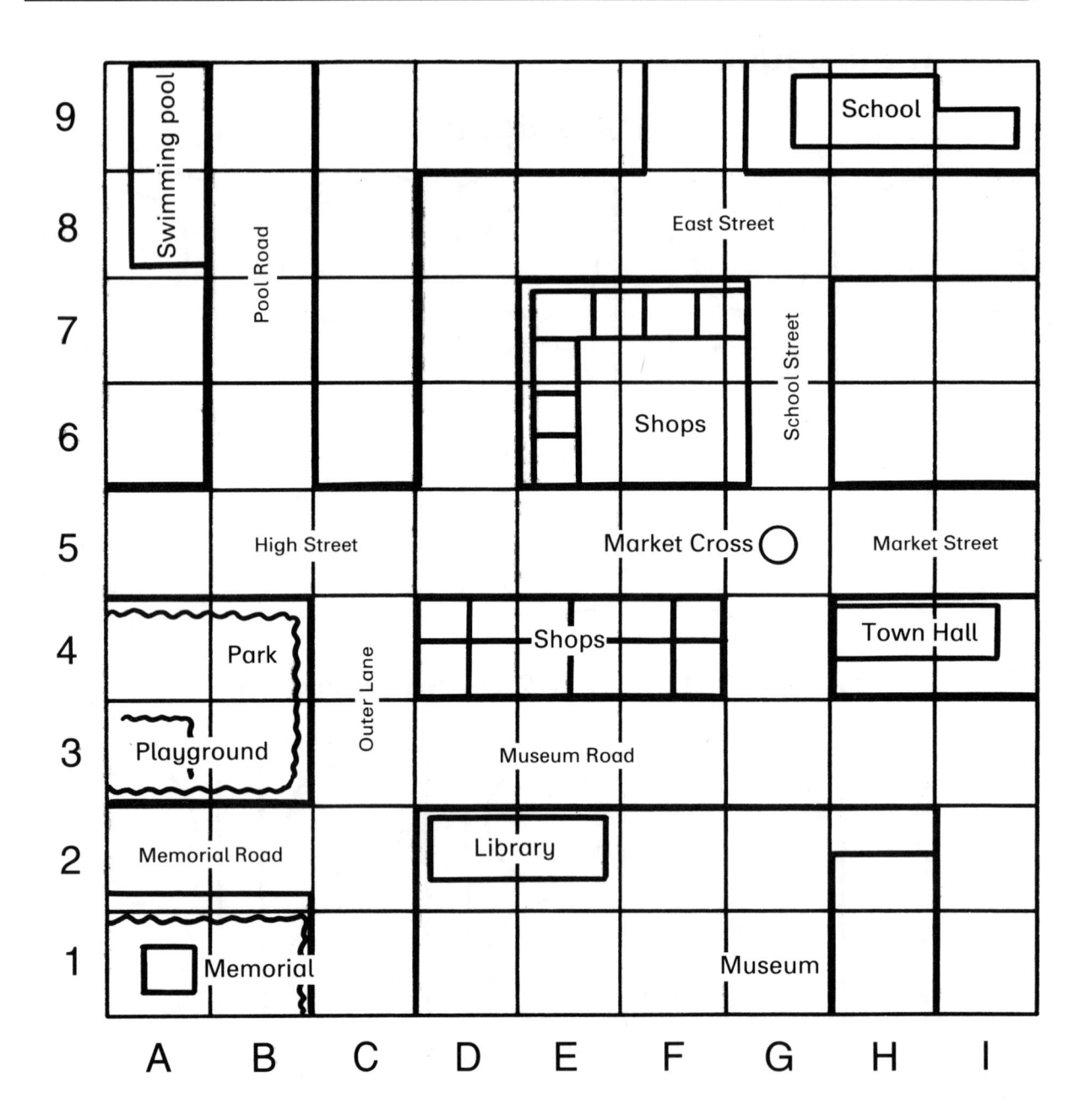

	A	B	C	D	E	F	G	H	I

9 — Swimming pool; School
8 — Pool Road; East Street
7 — School Street
6 — Shops
5 — High Street; Market Cross ○; Market Street
4 — Park; Shops; Town Hall
3 — Playground; Outer Lane; Museum Road
2 — Memorial Road; Library
1 — Memorial; Museum

Write a guide to the centre of this town. Give the town a name and work out a walk taking in all the main buildings. Include a Key giving the map references of the buildings.

Find a guide book to a big town or city near your school. Find the location of some important buildings there on a map.

Copymaster 25

Name _____

Level 3/4: Shape, space & measures

Polyominoes

Pentominoes

Penta means five. Pentomino squares must touch.

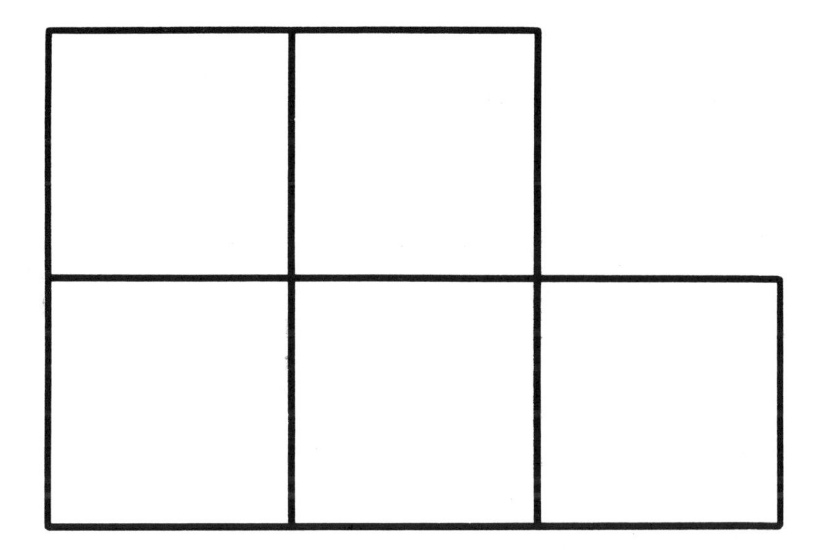

Use 1 inch squared paper. Draw and cut out as many different shapes as you can which use five squares.

How many are there? ☐

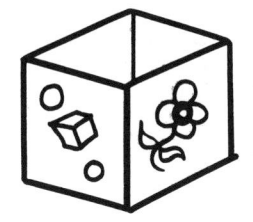

How many fold into a box open at the top? ☐

Make some hexominoes

Hexa means six. Hexomino squares must touch.

How many patterns can you find? ☐

How many fold into a box with a lid? ☐

Copymaster 26

Name _____

Level 3/4: Shape, space & measures

Möbius band

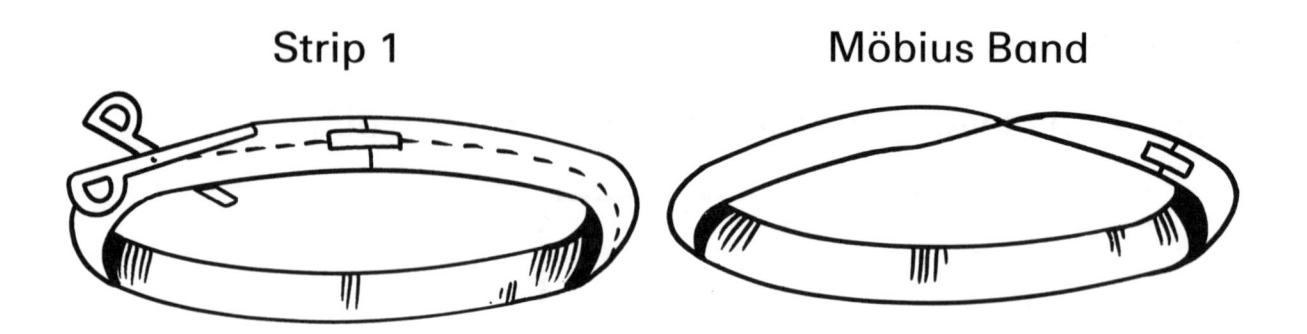

Strip 1   Möbius Band

Using 5mm squared paper cut out three strips, each 28cm long and 3 cm wide.

Strip 1
Colour one side by rubbing it with a wax crayon.
Stick the ends together with Sellotape® to make a loop.
Now cut the strip along its length.
What happens?

Strip 2
Colour one side.
Stick the ends together giving the strip one twist.
This is a Möbius Band.
Now cut the strip along its length.
What happens?

Strip 3
Colour one side.
Stick the ends together to make a Möbius Band.
Cut all the way around the strip at 1 cm away from the edge.
You should find you can cut twice around the band.
What happens?

Experiment with longer strips to make bands with more twists and wider strips so that you can cut $\frac{1}{4}$ or $\frac{1}{5}$ from the edge.

Copymaster 27

Name _____

Level 3/4: Shape, space & measures

Measures 2 (1 of 2)

Talk about and write notes on all the things you would need to find out to work out these problems and the measuring instruments you would use.

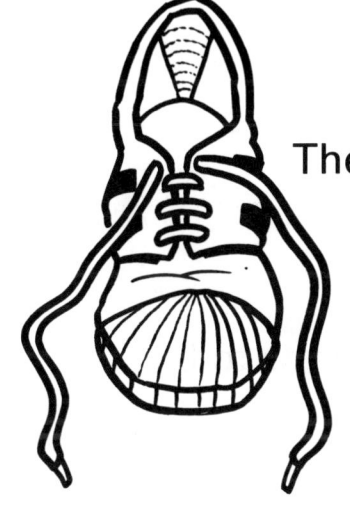

The best length for a trainer lace.

The best size for a logo and address on printed stationery.

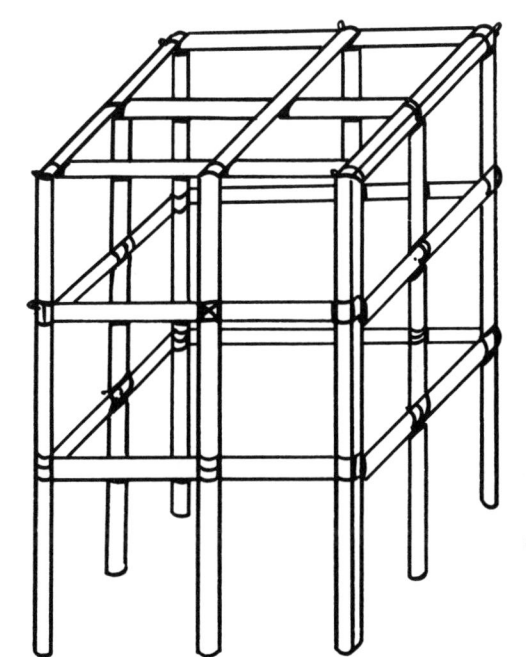

The dimensions for a playground climbing frame.

Copymaster 28

Name _____

Level 3/4: Shape, space & measures

Measures 2 (2 of 2)

Talk about and write notes on all the things you would need to find out to work out these problems and the measuring instruments you would use.

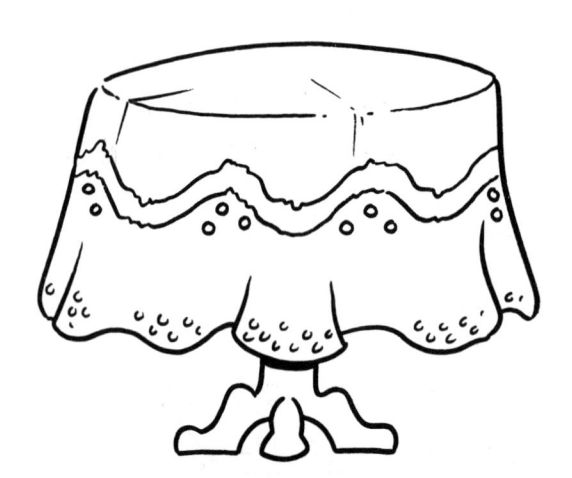

The size a four-cup teapot needs to be.

The dimensions of a tablecloth for a round table.

How many balls of wools will make a jumper.

Copymaster 29

Name _____

Level 3/4: Number/Handling data

Dominoes

How many dominoes in a set?

Count and record the total number of dots on each domino.

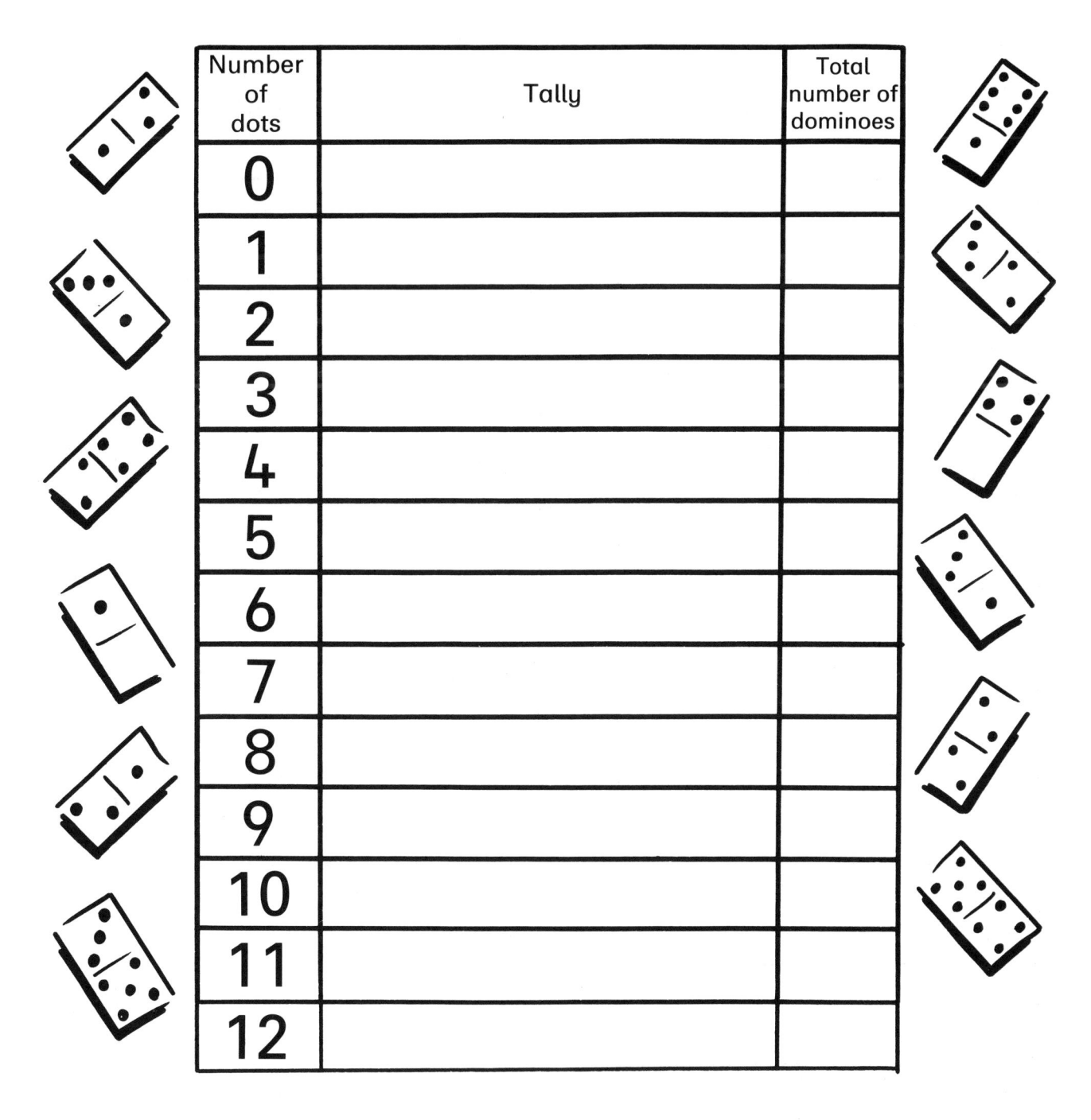

Number of dots	Tally	Total number of dominoes
0		
1		
2		
3		
4		
5		
6		
7		
8		
9		
10		
11		
12		

Make a picture to show the pattern of the tally.
What will the picture look like if there are 0–10 dots on each domino? Or if there are 0–12 dots on each domino?

Copymaster 30

Name _____   Level 3/4: Shape, space & measures

24 hours

Draw what you do in a day and a night.

Cut out and glue.

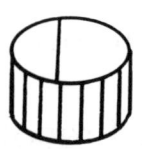

Midday

12, 11, 10, 9, 8, 7, 6, 5, 4, 3, 2, 1

Midnight

12, 11, 10, 9, 8, 7, 6, 5, 4, 3, 2, 1

Count the hours you spend sleeping, at school and playing.

Copymaster 31

Name _____

Level 3/4: Number/Shape, space & measures

Windscreen wipers

Stay safe.

Check with your teacher, headteacher and caretaker about working in the car park.

Choose three cars in the school car park.

Find out which car has the most effective windscreen wiper(s).

Talk about the problem first. Write down the measuring tools you need and the measurements you will take.

Copymaster 32

Name _____

Level 3/4: Number

Triangular numbers

Lay out some counters to make triangles that get bigger and bigger.

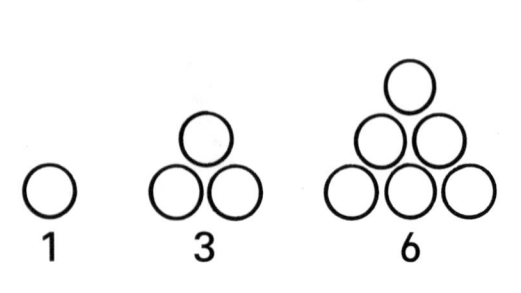

1   3   6

triangular numbers

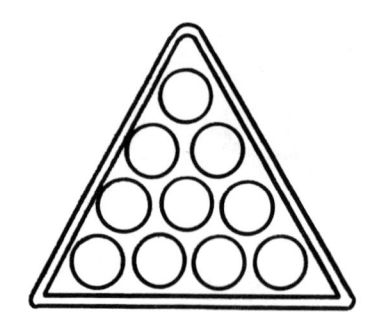

How many counters do you need to add on each time?

Write the triangular numbers up to 55.

How many counters are in each row to make the triangular number 55?

Show how successive triangular numbers can be made from a triangular number added to a natural number; and how square numbers can be made by adding two triangular numbers.

Natural Numbers   1 + 2   3   4   5   6   7   8   9   10

Triangular Numbers   1 + 3   6

Square Numbers   1   4   9

Copymaster 33

Name _____   Level 3/4: Number

Square numbers

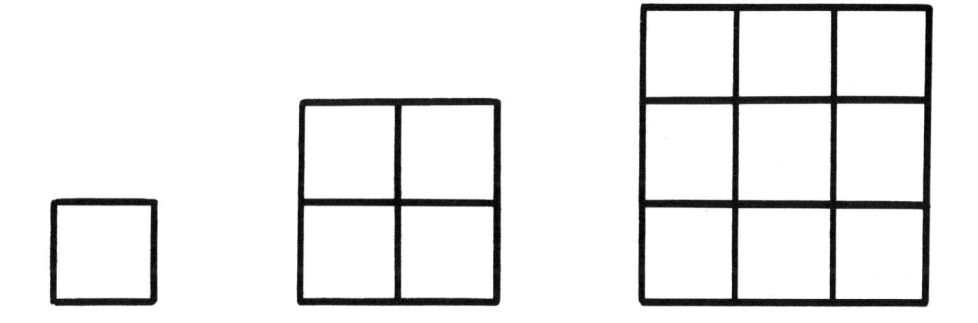

Use cubes or squared paper to make a series of squares which get bigger and bigger.

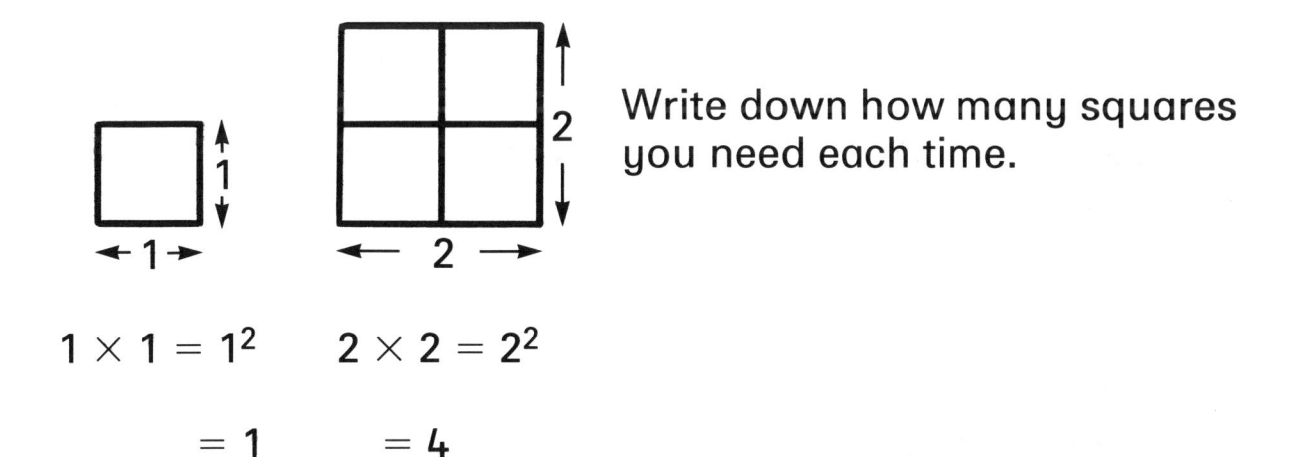

Write down how many squares you need each time.

$1 \times 1 = 1^2$ $2 \times 2 = 2^2$

$ = 1$ $ = 4$

How many do you need to add to make the next square? Write down the pattern of the number of squares you need to add on.

Use this pattern to work out how you can predict the answer to the sum of a series of odd numbers starting with 1.

Copymaster 34

Name _____

Level 3/4: Number

Palindromes

Palindromic number sequences read the same from either end.

11 × 11 = 121

111 × 111 = 12321

What other palindromes can you find by multiplying?

1991 and 2002 are palindromic years. Find some others.

3 September 1993 written 3.9.93 is palindromic.
Find some others.

Record some palindromic dates in history and the events that happened on those dates.

Copymaster 35

Name _____

Level 3/4: Number

Best buy

20p 13p 60p 50p 5p 35p 10p

90p   £5   £4·20   £1·25   £2·50

10p   20p   30p   40p   50p   £1

£1·50   £1·75   £2·25   £2·75   £3·20

| £1·50 | £17·36 | £94·23 | £102·06 | £84·01 | £110·10 |
| £75·67 | £2·99 | £61·17 | £50·84 | £32·19 | £4·44 |

Copymaster 36

Name _____

Level 3/4: Number

Think of a number

Think of a number *Ping*

Double it
Add 20
Divide by 2
Take away 9
Take away your starting number

The answer is ...

1

Does it always work?
How does it work?
Is the order important?

Think of a number
× 4
+ 200

Halve the answer
− 100
÷ 2

What do you get?

Now try this one

Can you change the puzzles and still make them work? Make up a 'Think of a number' puzzle.

Copymaster 37

Name _____

Level 3/4: Number

Story of 2

Find out about 2.

Copymaster 38

Name _____

Level 3/4: Handling data

Questionnaire

What is the title of a book you are reading or have just read?

What do you think of the book?

Will you read more by the same author?

Which three books are your all-time favourites?

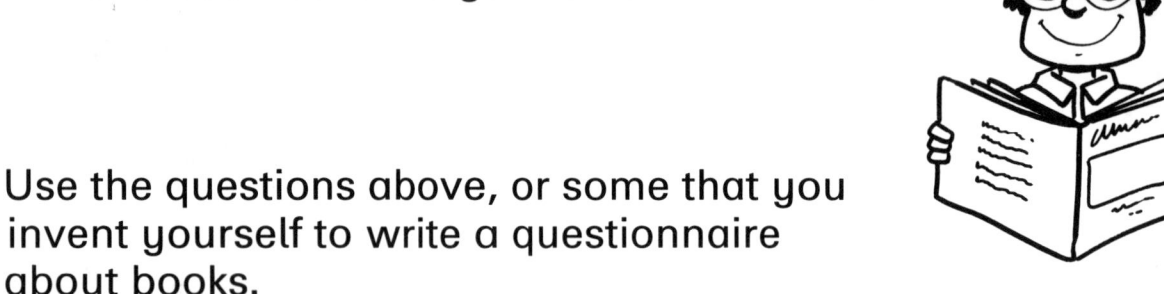

Use the questions above, or some that you invent yourself to write a questionnaire about books.

Ask ten people in your school these questions. Talk about what can be done with the replies. Say what questions gave you problems and why.

Now make up your own questionnaire about a topic of your choice. Ask people to answer your questions. Report on what you did and what the results were.

Record some 'golden rules' for anyone who wants to invent a questionnaire.

Golden rule 1.

Golden rule 2.

Golden rule 3.

Copymaster 39

Name _____

Level 3/4: Shape, space & measures

Symmetry: Badges

Look for badges, emblems, flags, logos and other things where the designs show symmetry.

Trace or copy them and make a chart useful to other children.

Design your own personal badge or logo here.

Make it show either reflectional or rotational symmetry or both.

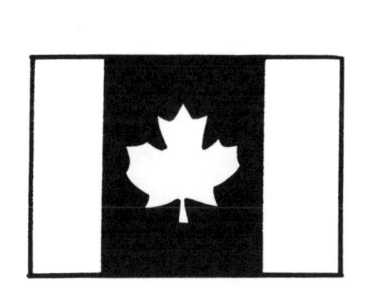

Copymaster 40

Name _____

Level 1/2: Number/Shape, space & measures/Handling data

Survey: Left and right

Which hand do you write with?
Which foot do you prefer to kick a ball with?

Ask 20 people.

Name	Hand L or R	Foot L or R

What fraction of people are left-handed?

What percentage are right-handed?

What percentage are right-handed *and* right-footed?

Copymaster 41

Name _____

Level 3/4: Shape, space & measures

Shapes in buildings: Making a trail

On a walk around the neighbourhood, look at the buildings. Spot the shapes including some of these:

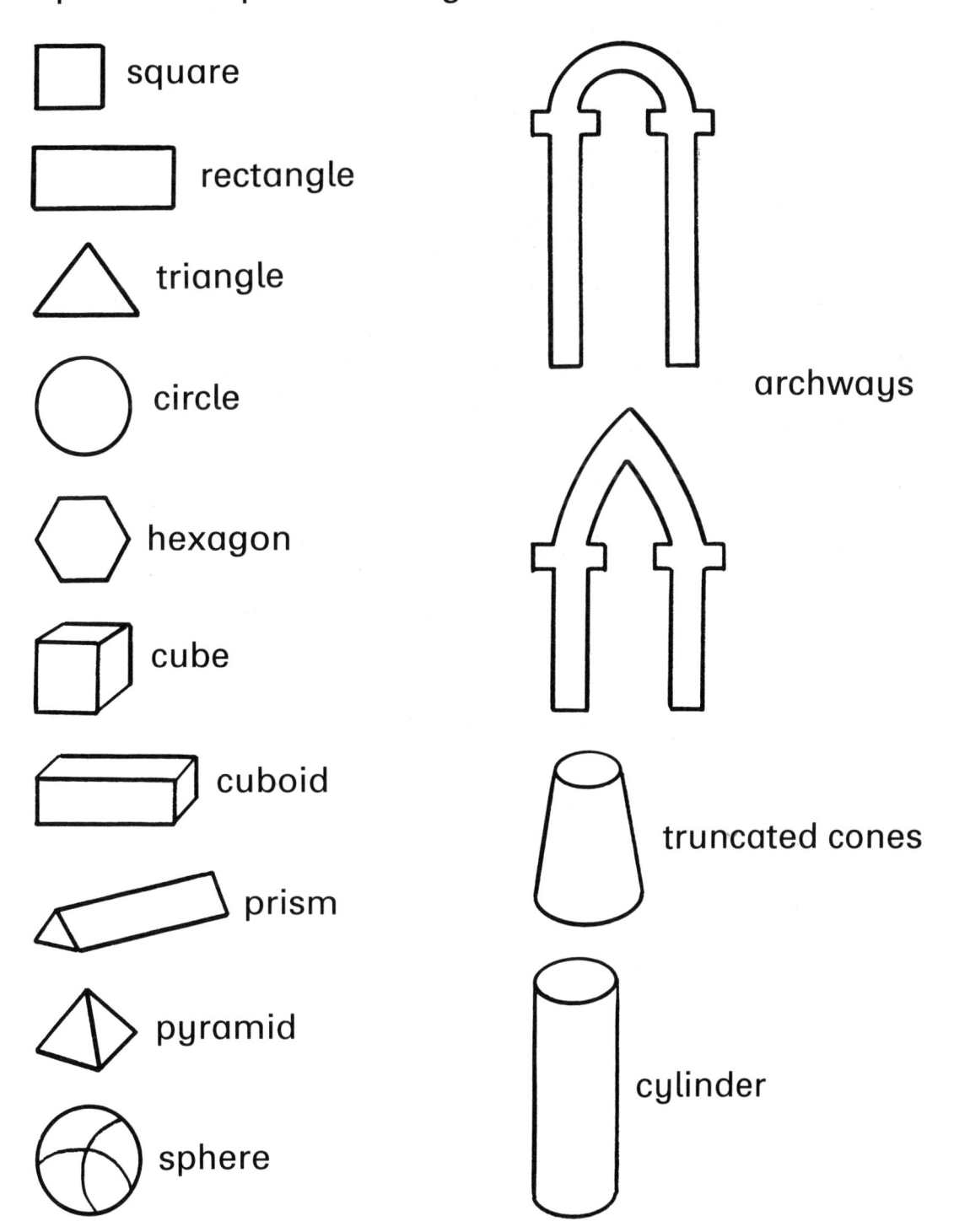

- square
- rectangle
- triangle
- circle
- hexagon
- cube
- cuboid
- prism
- pyramid
- sphere

- archways
- truncated cones
- cylinder

On the reverse side of this sheet draw a rough sketch of a trail, marking in where the shapes occur.

Make a good copy of your sketch, naming roads and some of the buildings so that other children can follow the trail.

Copymaster 42

Name _____

Level 3/4: Number

Prime numbers

1	2	3	4	5	6	7	8	9	10
11									

Eratosthenes was a Greek astronomer and mathematician who proposed a way to 'sieve' out prime numbers. Here is how to do it. Fill in the numbers on the 100 square.

- Leave 1 as it is. It is a rather special number.
- 2 can only be divided by 1 and itself so it is a prime number.

Put a ring round it. Now cross out all the other multiples of 2 (that is 4, 6, 8, 10 and so on).

They cannot be prime as they have the factor 2.

- 3 can only be divided by 1 and itself. Put a ring round it. Cross out all the multiples of 3.

- 4 is already crossed out.

- ← Look at 5 ... go through this task for all the times tables until all the numbers are ringed (Primes) or crossed out (not Primes).

List all the prime numbers to 100 here.

Look at the list. What can you say about:
- All the prime numbers (except 2)?
- The number before or after each prime (except 2 and 3)?

Copymaster 43

Name _____

Level 3/4: Shape, space & measures

Mazes (1 of 2)

Cut out these tiles. Use some of them to make a maze.

Find a picture of a real maze. Use these tiles or some you design yourself to make a copy of it.

Copymaster 44

Name _____

Level 3/4: Shape, space & measures

Mazes (2 of 2)

Maze tile blanks.

Copymaster 45

Name _____

Level 3/4: Number

Function machines: trail

A function machine does the same thing to any input number.

This is an add five machine [+ 5]

Find the output

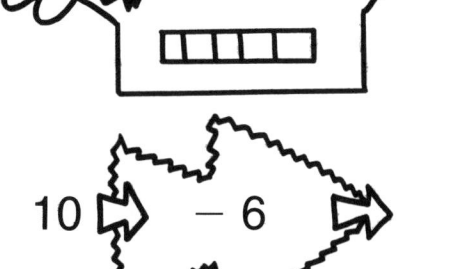

2 → + 2 →

4 → × 4 →

10 → − 6 →

Find the input

→ ÷ 2 → 6

→ + 10 → 20

→ × 5 → 30

6 → ÷ 3 → × 12 → × 2 → − 8 → ÷ 10 → ÷ 7 → − 23 → × 11 → + 15 → □

Invent your own function machine trail.

Copymaster 46

Name _____

Level 3/4: Number

Function machines: challenges

A function machine performs the same maths operation on any input number

Work out two different ways each of these machines may be working

                                 Way 1   Way 2

12 → 6

9 → 17

18 → 7

8 → 16

4 → 24

25 → 5

Copymaster 47

Name _____

Level 3/4: Handling data

Drinks survey

Find out which drink tastes best and which costs least.

Make up some orange squash and put into cups marked S
Squeeze the fresh oranges and pour into cups marked O
Pour out some orange juice from a carton into cups marked J

Ask ten people to taste and rate these drinks:

* poor   ** OK   *** tasty   **** very good   ***** delicious

Name of tester	Squash (S)	Squeezed orange (O)	Orange juice from carton (J)

Total number of stars   ____   ____   ____

What does 30 mls of each drink cost?   squash ☐

orange juice from carton ☐   squeezed orange ☐

Tastiest drink

Cheapest drink

Copymaster 48

Name _____

Level 3/4: Number

Polybius checkerboard code

The Polybius Checkerboard

	1	2	3	4	5
1	a	b	c	d	e
2	f	g	h	i	j
3	k	l	m	n	o
4	p	q	r	s	t
5	uv	w	x	y	z

To change the word 'secret' into numbers use the numerals in the rows and columns:

letter	row	column	code
s	4	4	44
e	1	5	15
c	1	3	13
r	4	3	43
e	1	5	15
t	4	5	45

The code for 'secret' is 44, 15, 13, 43, 15, 45
Write some coded messages to a classmate. Use these and your friend's replies to make a book.

Copymaster 49

Name _____

Level 3/4: Number

Finding out about numbers

Choose a number 3, 5, 7 or 13.

Look for all the stories, rhymes, songs, chants, sayings and superstitions about your number.
Write a report or poem telling all your discoveries.

Copymaster 50

Name _____

Level 3/4: Number

Calendar month

Copy the dates of any calendar month onto the diagram. Choose and draw round a square of four numbers. (An example square is shown.)

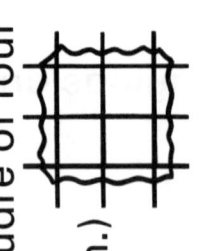

Add the diagonals …
Try this with other squares of four numbers.
Multiply the smallest number of the four numbers by the next smallest and add 16.
Then add all four numbers together …

Now draw around a square of nine numbers. Add the diagonals.

Add the numbers in the middle column (↑). Add the numbers in the middle row (→).

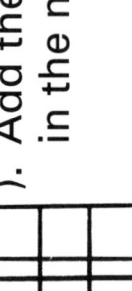

Total the corner numbers and divide the total by the centre number. Try all these for other squares of nine numbers. Look for more patterns in a calendar month.

Mon	Tues	Wed	Thurs	Fri	Sat	Sun

Copymaster 51

Name _____

Level 3/4: Shape, space & measures

Tangrams

A tangram: An ancient Chinese puzzle

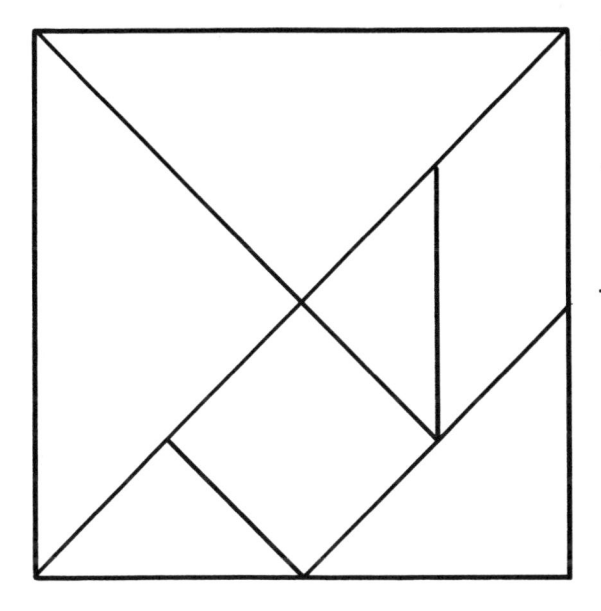

Cut out the pieces of the tangram. Use all seven to make pictures.

- Try making a man, a boat, a fish or bird
- Make the square you started with

Lay your pieces on these outlines to make:

a rectangle

a parallelogram

Can you also make a triangle or a trapezium using all seven pieces?

Make a collage using tangram pictures.

Copymaster 52

Name _____

Level 3/4: Shape, space & measures

Symmetry: Letters and numerals

Find and draw all the letters of the alphabet that show reflective and/or rotational symmetry. Use capitals - e.g. A

A B C D E F G H I J K L M N O P Q R S T U V W X Y Z 0 1 2 3 4 5 6 7 8 9

Letters showing reflective symmetry

Letters showing rotational symmetry

Letters showing both reflective and rotational symmetry.

Now try the numerals 0–9

Show reflective symmetry   Show rotational symmetry

Show both reflective and rotational symmetry

Copymaster 53

Name _____

Level 3/4: Shape, space & measures

Tiles (1 of 2)

Choose a pattern for a tile or invent one of your own.

Try making a pattern using translation

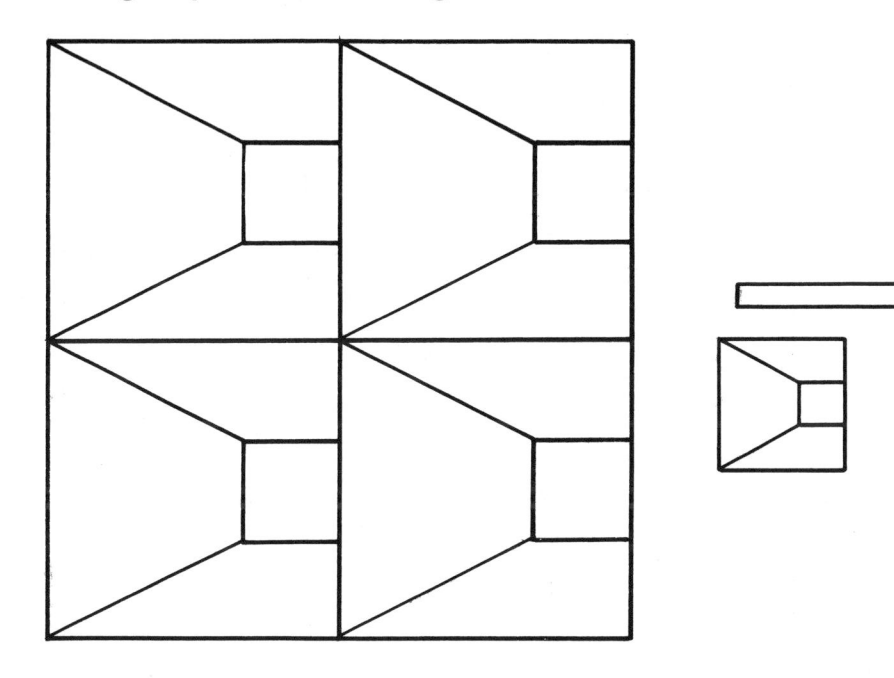

Try making a pattern using rotation

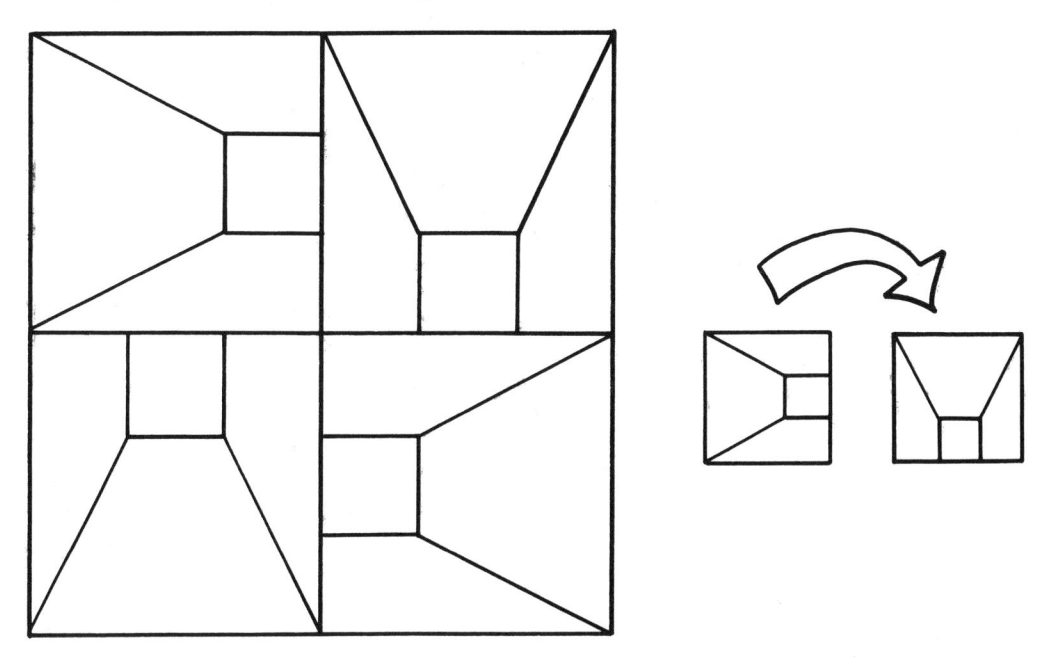

Colour and decorate your pattern.

Copymaster 54

Name _____

Level 3/4: Shape, space & measures

Tiles (2 of 2)

Choose a pattern.

Copymaster 55

Name _____

Level 3/4: Number

9 × table and dividing by 9

Write out the 9 × table.

0 × 9 =	
1 × 9 =	

What happens when you add the numerals in each product to make its reduced number?

Look at the pattern of products. Is there a point where the pattern changes?

'Casting out nines'

Write down a three-digit number.

Find its reduced number.

Divide the starting number by 9.

What is the remainder?

Try this with other numbers.

How can you find the remainder easily?

Copymaster 56

Name _____

Level 3/4: Number

Addition squares

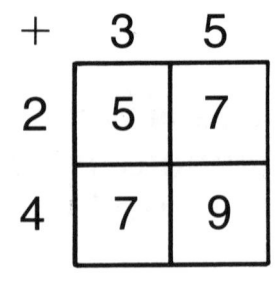

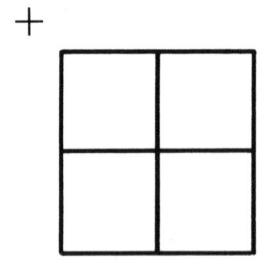

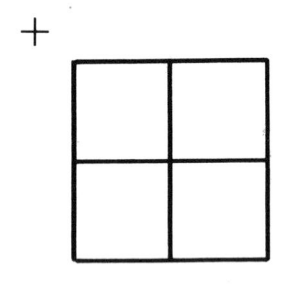

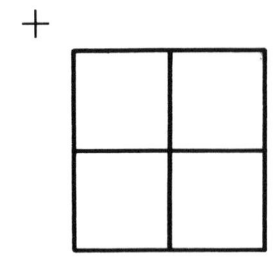

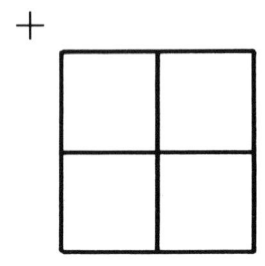

+	3	5
2	5	7
4	7	9

+	6	7
6		
7		

Try these addition squares. What patterns can you find? The first one is done for you. Look at the sum of the diagonal numbers, the sum of all the numbers put into the square (2 + 4 + 3 + 5), and look at the bottom left and top right numbers.

Fill in the other squares and look for more patterns. Then draw some squares of your own.

Copymaster 57

Name _____

Level 3/4: Number

Calculator challenge

The Code

A	B	C	D	E	F	G	H	I	J	K	L	M
1	2	3	4	5	6	7	8	9	10	11	12	13

N	O	P	Q	R	S	T	U	V	W	X	Y	Z
14	15	16	17	18	19	20	21	22	23	24	25	26

Write your name in code.

What is the sum of the letters?

What is the product when you multiply the initials of your first name and surname together?

What is the highest number you can make by totalling the letters in a three letter word?

What is the lowest scoring three letter word?

Try multiplying the sums of the letters of two words. Make the biggest total you can.

Reverse the code making A = 26, B = 25

What is the highest addition total you can make with a word of six letters?

What is the lowest addition total you can make with a word of four letters?

Copymaster 58

Name _____

Level 3/4: Number

Magic square

This is a magic square. Add the rows, columns and diagonals … magic!

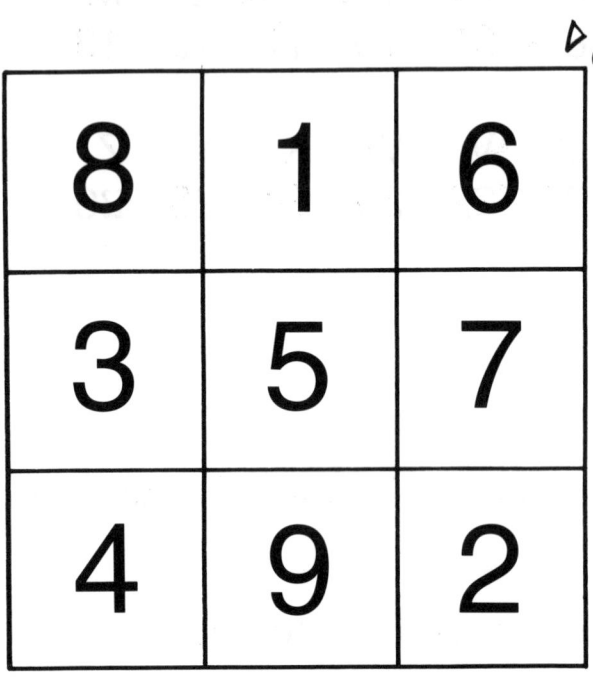

8	1	6
3	5	7
4	9	2

Compare these numbers with those above and fill in the rest of the numbers to make another magic square.

13		
	10	

Try making 4 × 4 (fourth order) and 5 × 5 (fifth order) magic squares.

Copymaster 59

Name _____   Level 5: Shape, space & measures

Pentagrams

The centre of a pentagram is a regular pentagon.

The points of a pentagram join to make a regular pentagon

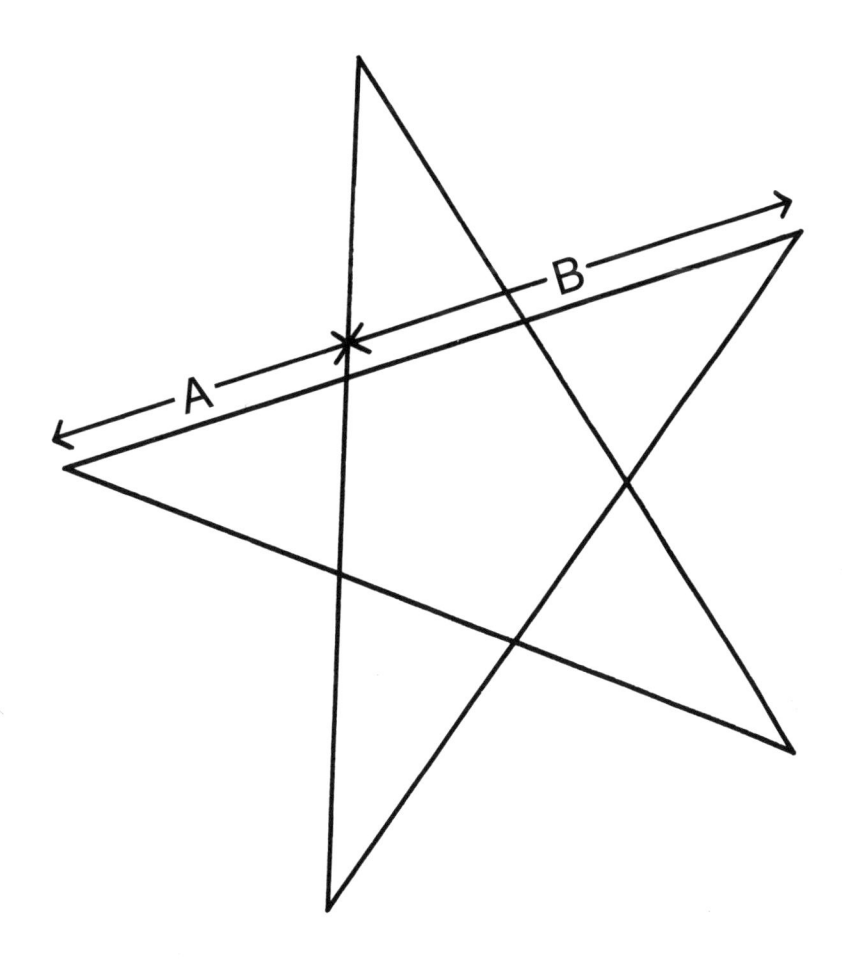

Measure A and B. Their ratio should be close to 1.618. This is the Golden Ratio. Look for the Golden Ratio in other parts of this pentagram. Now draw your own pentagram, starting with a regular pentagon. Look for Golden Ratios in its measurements.

Copymaster 60

Name _____   Level 5: Number/Shape, space & measures

Make a newsletter

Make a collection of newspapers, comics and magazines. Compare them in all the ways you can. Here are some ways to compare them:

- Style and presentation
- Number of photographs compared with amount of print
- Margins and column width
- Size of headlines
- Kind of type used and sizes of type
- Proportions of each paper given to different kinds of news.

Using copies of a local newspaper, comics or magazines choose some items for a newsletter.

Photocopy the items, enlarging and reducing the print to fit a layout you have designed.

Make up the layout and display it in the classroom.

Copymaster 61

Name _____   Level 5: Number/Shape, space & measures

Furniture design

Design a chair and table that is comfortable for someone of average height and build in your class.

To start
1. Decide which measurements will give you the average height and build.
2. Measure a sample of people.
3. Calculate the average measurements.

Go on
4. Choose someone who is close in actual measurements to the class average.
5. Decide which measurements you need to help with your design. For example, you may need height when seated, from bottom to eye-level.
6. Take those measures of your sample average person.

Finally
7. Decide on a scale for drawings you make.
8. Make rough sketches.
9. Draw the final designs.
10. Report on why the design would be comfortable.

Copymaster 62

Name _____

Level 5: Shape, space & measures

Classroom planner

Draw a classroom layout

Pushing back chairs . Room to move . Remember .

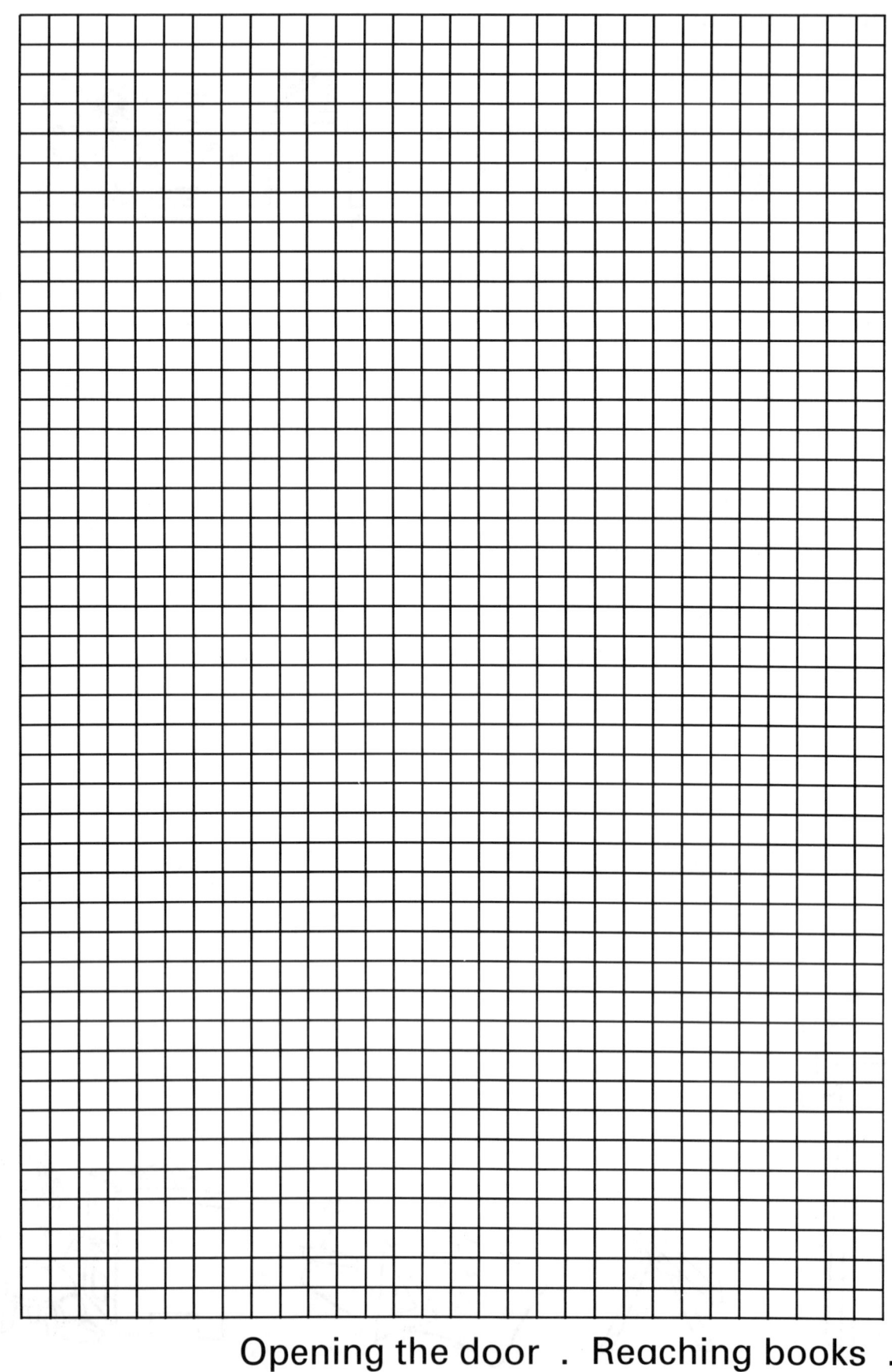

Remember . Access to cupboards . Seeing the computer .

Opening the door . Reaching books .

Copymaster 63

Name _____

Level 5: Number/Handling data

Vedic square

This is an ancient Hindu multiplication square which produces symmetrical patterns.

The square is made by multiplying the numbers in the rows and columns.

When the answer is more than nine the digits are added together until nine or less is obtained.

For example: $6 \times 3 = 18 \rightarrow 1 + 8 = 9$ 9 goes in the 6×3 cell

$7 \times 7 = 49 \rightarrow 4 + 9 = 13$ $1 + 3 = 4$ 4 goes in the 7×7 cell

Make a vedic square using squared paper. Choose a number and connect all the cells with that number together. Each number gives a pattern. Here are the 6s and 3s. They look alike except one pattern has been rotated.

x	1	2	3	4	5	6	7	8	9
1	1	2	3	4	5	6	7	8	9
2	2	4	6	8	1	3	5	7	9
3	3	6	9	3	6	9	3	6	9
4	4	8	3	7	2	6	1	5	9
5	5	1	6	2	7	3	8	4	9
6	6	3	9	6	3	9	6	3	9
7	7	5	3	1	8	6	4	2	9
8	8	7	6	5	4	3	2	1	9
9	9	9	9	9	9	9	9	9	9

x	1	2	3	4	5	6	7	8	9
1	1	2	3	4	5	6	7	8	9
2	2	4	6	8	1	3	5	7	9
3	3	6	9	3	6	9	3	6	9
4	4	8	3	7	2	6	1	5	9
5	5	1	6	2	7	3	8	4	9
6	6	3	9	6	3	9	6	3	9
7	7	5	3	1	8	6	4	2	9
8	8	7	6	5	4	3	2	1	9
9	9	9	9	9	9	9	9	9	9

The pattern can be copied to make a tile.

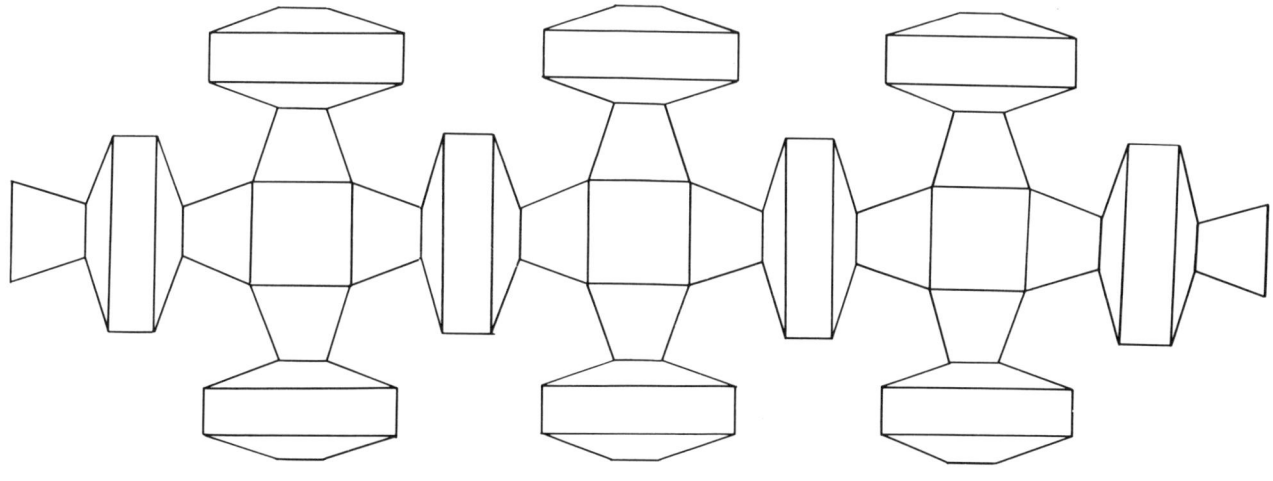

Make a tile using your number pattern.

Copymaster 64

Name _____

Level 5: Number/Handling data

Pascal's triangle: Patterns in the triangle

```
1
1  1
1  2   1
1  3   3   1
1  4   6   4   1
1  5  10  10   5   1
1  6  15  20  15   6   1
1  7  21  35  35  21   7   1
1  8  28  56  70  56  28   8   1
```

Look for the patterns in Pascal's Triangle.
For example, can you see:
1 2 3 4 ... count in ones
1 3 6 10 ... triangular numbers

Write down some more of the patterns you find
From the diagonals can you make the Fibonacci Series
1 1 2 3 5 8 13 21 ...

Copymaster 65

Name _____

Level 5: Number/Handling data

Pascal's triangle: Spiders and elevens

Eight spiders on a trellis three panels high.
They split into two equal groups and go down the seam of the trellis only to split again into equal groups at the next junction.

How many spiders come out at each seam at the bottom?

Try it yourself with 16 or 32 spiders.

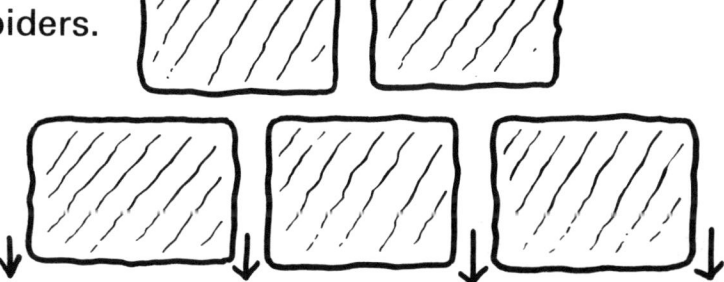

Draw a diagram here.

How many layers of trellis did you need?

Write in: 11 =   11 × 11 =   11 × 11 × 11 =   11 × 11 × 11 × 11 =

How does this link with the spiders on the trellis?

Copymaster 66

Name _____

Level 5: Number/Handling data

Pascal's triangle: Coin toss

List the numbers of possible results if you tossed some coins.

2 coins

3 coins

4 coins

Can you predict what the pattern of possible outcomes will be for more coins?

Copymaster 67

Name _____

Level 5: Number/Shape, space & measures

Fibonacci series

Write two 1s on the dotted line in the box below. Add the 1s together and write the total (2) next to the two 1s.
Add the last number (2) to the number before it (1) and write this number next.
Continue doing this to produce the Fibonacci Series.

Find the ratio of some of the pairs of numbers
8:13
13:21

Choose some more ...

What do you notice about all the ratios?

Copymaster 68

Name _____   Level 5: Number/Shape, space & measures

Fibonacci: Golden ratio

Make a collection of pieces of paper of different standard sizes. Two examples are A4 and foolscap. For each piece work out the ratio of width to length.

Paper sample number	Width	Length	Ratio width:length

Find out the actual measurements of some famous paintings. Work out the ratio of width to length.

Title of painting	Name of artist	Width	Length	Ratio width:length

Now compare some of the measurements in pictures of Greek sculptures.

Talk about your findings.

Copymaster 69

Name _____

Level 5: Number/Shape, space & measures

Fibonacci: Spirals

1 unit

Work out the relationship of the sides of the squares in these diagrams.

Using a large sheet of paper, or a broad piece of chalk on the playground, go on extending the size of the squares until you have no more room. Draw in the spiral.

Spirals occur in the natural world. Examples include:
• daisy heads   • pine cones   • shells   • horns   • pineapples.
Add some more examples here:

Find out how these natural spirals are linked to the Fibonacci Series.

Copymaster 70

Name _____

Level 5: Number

Multiplication squares and patterns

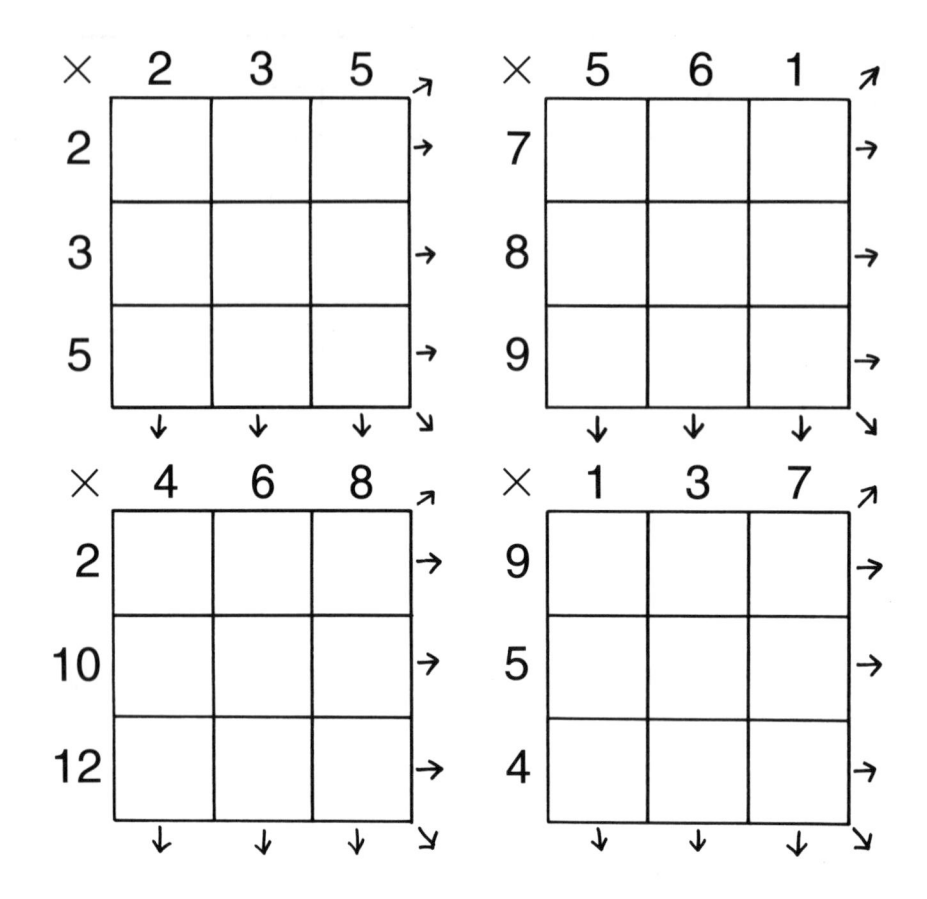

×	2	3	5
2			
3			
5			

×	5	6	1
7			
8			
9			

×	4	6	8
2			
10			
12			

×	1	3	7
9			
5			
4			

Fill in the squares. Add up the rows, columns and diagonals (✗).
Try some more of you own. Are there general rules which help you predict some of the answers?

Some multiplication tables make patterns if you look at the last digit in each answer. Here is the 6 × table

0 × 6   0
1 × 6   6
2 × 6   12
3 × 6   18
4 × 6   24
5 × 6   30
6 × 6   36
7 × 6   42
8 × 6   48
9 × 6   54
10 × 6   60

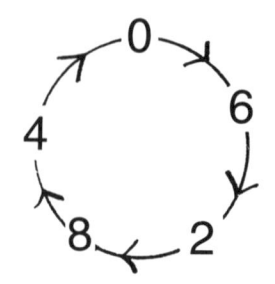

Look at other tables to see if there are patterns.

Copymaster 71

Name _____   Level 5: Handling data

Music by chance

Write down any three notes you can play (for example on the recorder or glockenspiel).
Now write the notes in all the possible orders. You should find there are six ways of writing them. Number these patterns one to six. Roll a die eight times, recording on plain paper or on the stave, the note patterns that match the number rolled on the die each time.
Play the tune.

Starting pattern of notes:

Note patterns:

If you had four notes in your original pattern, how many possible patterns of notes would there be?

What are the numbers of possible patterns with five notes? Six notes?

Copymaster 72

Name _____

Level 5: Number/Shape, space & measures

Angles

Find the totals of the internal angles and external angles of the shapes. What do you notice?

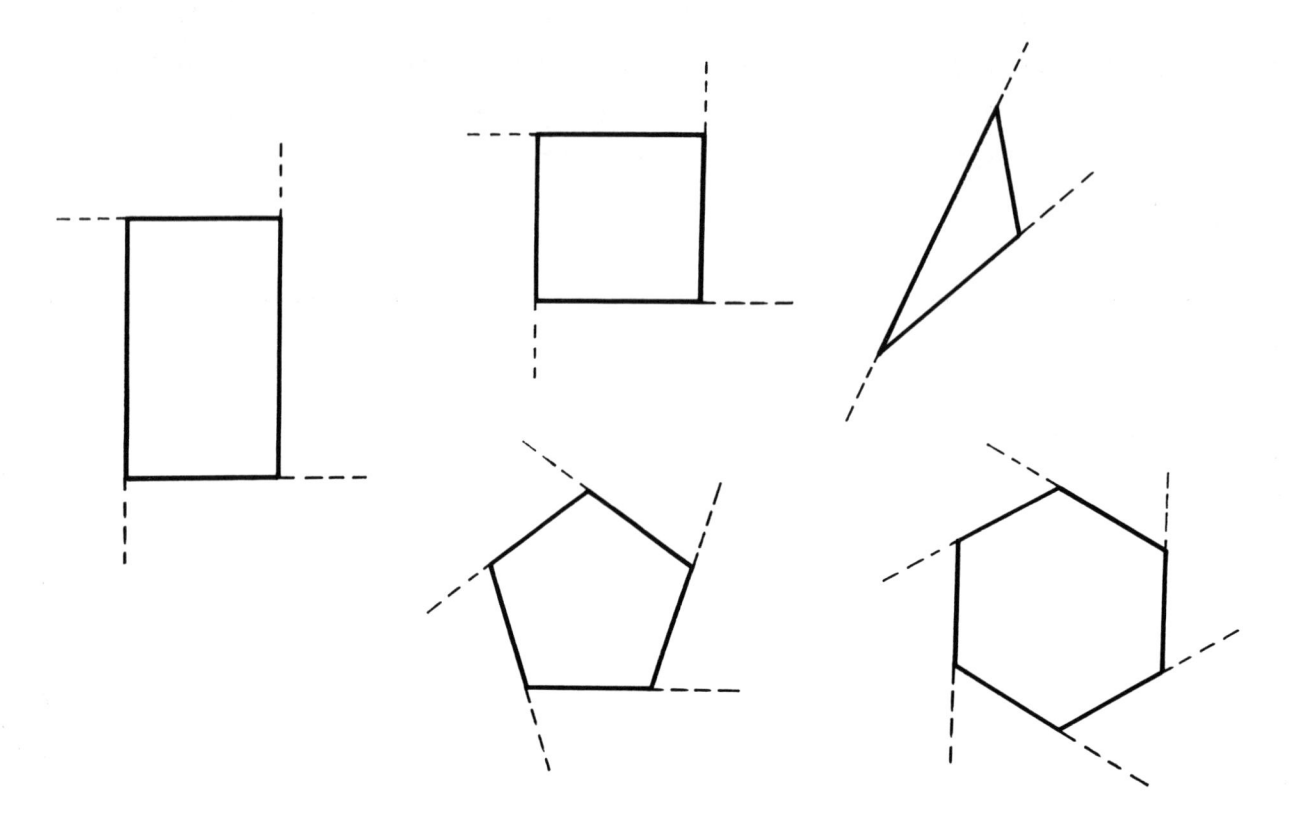

Try some more shapes. Test out what you have found.

Copymaster 73

Name _____

Level 5: Number/Shape, space & measures

Euler's relation

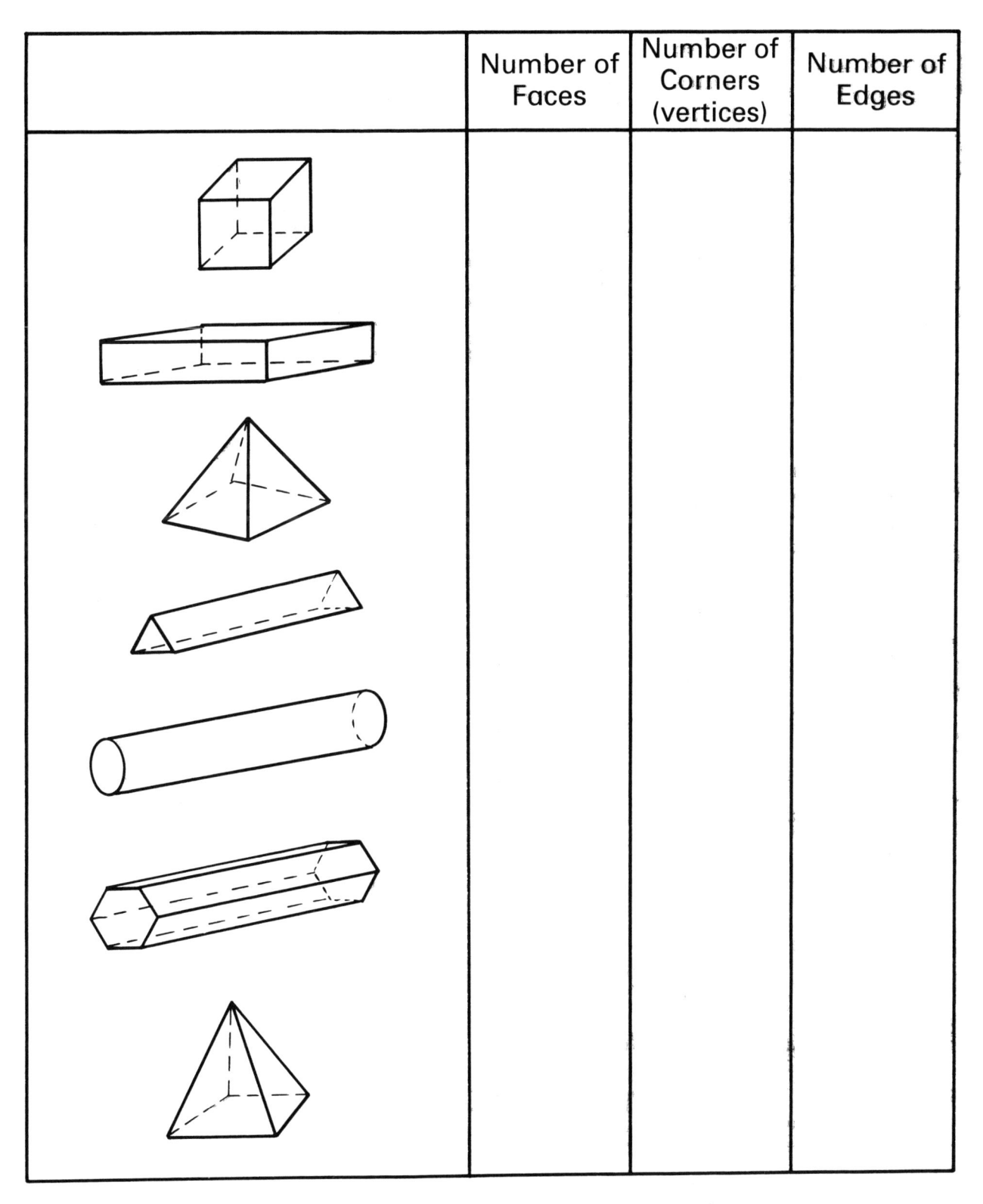

	Number of Faces	Number of Corners (vertices)	Number of Edges

Find a pattern to link faces, vertices and edges.

Copymaster 74

Name _____

Level 5: Number/Handling data

Handshakes

Pretend there are some people at a party.
If everyone shakes hands with everyone else, work out how many handshakes for the numbers of guests below:

Number of people	Number of handshakes
1	0
2	1
3	
4	
5	
6	
7	
8	

Talk about the pattern.

Copymaster 75

Name _____

Level 5: Shape, space & measures

Tessellation: Pictures

Cut out a 3 cm square or 3 cm equilateral triangle.

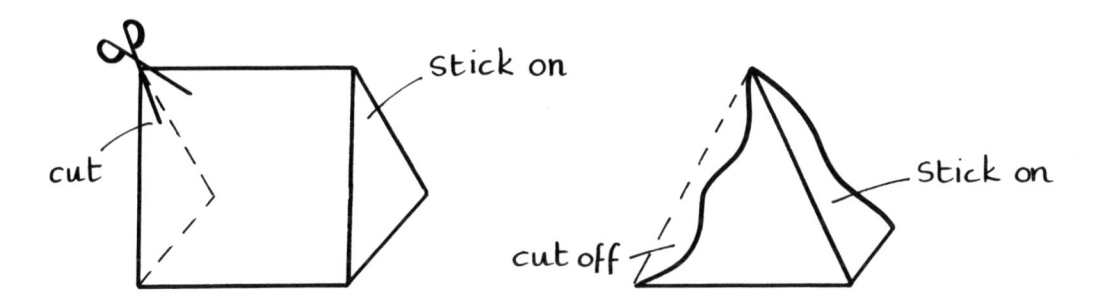

Cut a piece - any shape out of one side.
Stick it on the other side.

Draw round your shape to make tessellating patterns.

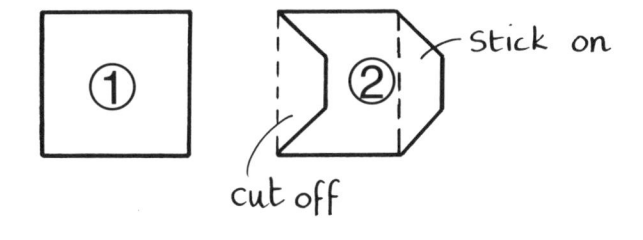

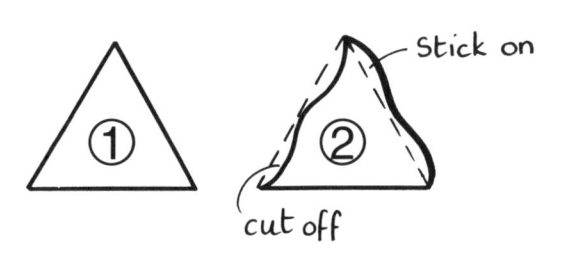

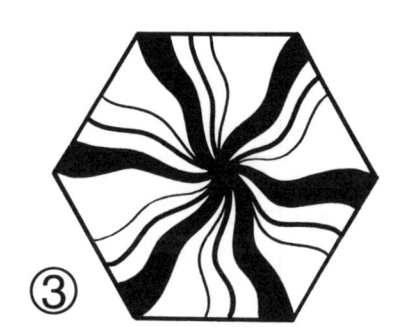

Copymaster 76

Name ______________________________

Napier's rods

Make the rods from lollystick or card strips.

0	1	2	3	4	5	6	7	8	9
0	1	2	3	4	5	6	7	8	9
0	2	4	6	8	1/0	1/2	1/4	1/6	1/8
0	3	6	9	1/2	1/5	1/8	2/1	2/4	2/7
0	4	8	1/2	1/6	2/0	2/4	2/8	3/2	3/6
0	5	1/0	1/5	2/0	2/5	3/0	3/5	4/0	4/5
0	6	1/2	1/8	2/4	3/0	3/6	4/2	4/8	5/4
0	7	1/4	2/1	2/8	3/5	4/2	4/9	5/6	6/3
0	8	1/6	2/4	3/2	4/0	4/8	5/6	6/4	7/2
0	9	1/8	2/7	3/6	4/5	5/4	6/3	7/2	8/1

2	5	8
2	5	8
4	1/0	1/6
6	1/5	2/4
8	2/0	3/2
1/0	2/5	4/0
1/2	3/0	4/8
1/4		5/6
1/6		6/4
1/8		7/2

Choose the rods that match the digits of a number

Here is the collection to match 258.
For multiples of this number look across the rods summing the diagonals.

← Thus $5 \times 258 = 1290$

← $6 \times 258 =$ | 1/2 | 3/0 | 4/8 |

$6 \times 258 =$ | 1/2 + 3/0 + 4/8 |

$= 1 \quad 5 \quad 4 \quad 8$

$= 1548$

Try some more yourself.

Name _____

Level 5: Number/Shape, space & measures

Perimeter and area

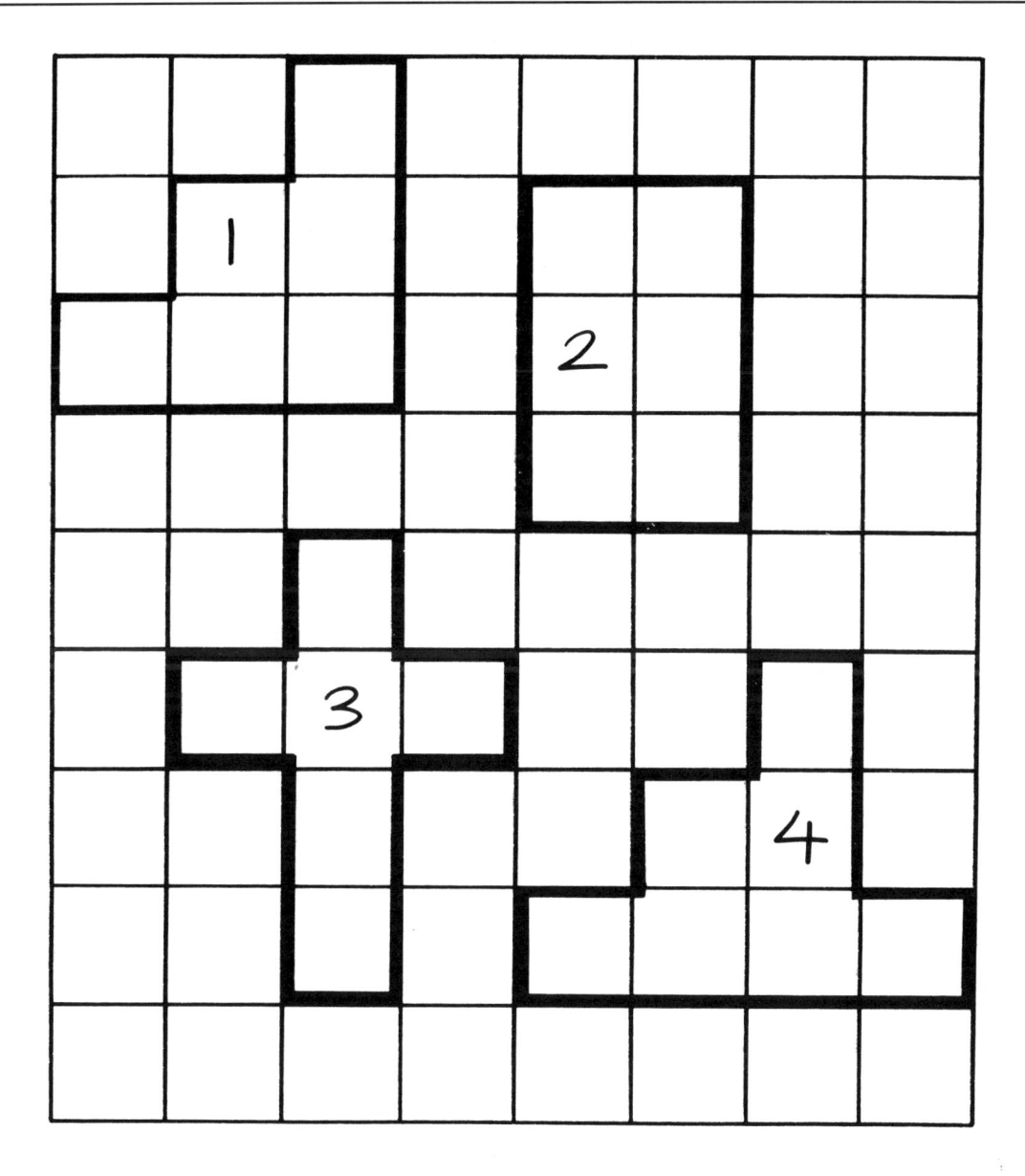

Using squared paper or a geoboard make some shapes which have the same area. Shapes 1 and 2 are both 6 squares. They have the same area.

Look at their perimeters.
Now make shapes which have different areas but the same perimeter.
Shapes 3 and 4 fit this pattern.

Copymaster 78

Name _____   Level 5: Number

The number 1089

Write down a three digit number.

Make sure the 'hundreds' are different from the 'units' by at least two.

Reverse the digits.

Subtract the smaller number from the larger one.

What do you get?

Reverse the digits. Add this number to the number you got. Total?

What is its reduced number?

Try again with some more three digit numbers.

1089

What results do you get with a four digit number?

Copymaster 79

Name _____

Level 5: Shape, space & measures

Snooker

Here is a three by two (3 × 2) imaginary snooker table.

Work out the route taken by a ball hit as shown in the picture (that is from one corner at 45°).

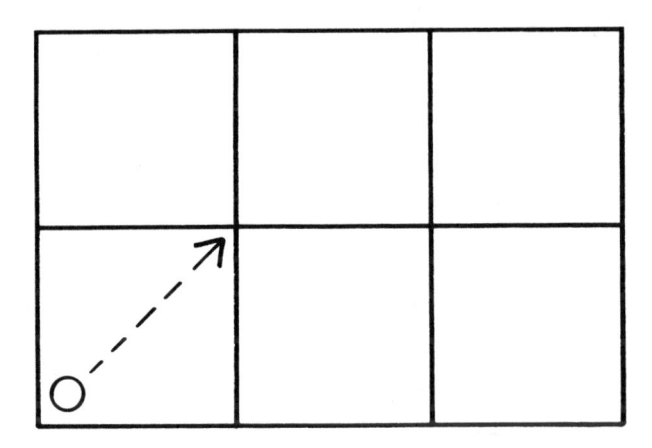

Imagine a number of snooker tables of different sizes, with four pockets only (one at each corner).

Using squared paper, draw tables of these sizes and draw in the ball's route. (The ball travels at 45° from the corner each time.)

$$3 \times 2 \qquad 4 \times 2 \qquad 5 \times 2$$

$$4 \times 4 \qquad 6 \times 6 \qquad 3 \times 7$$

$$4 \times 1 \qquad 5 \times 1 \qquad 10 \times 1$$

Look at how many times the ball crosses the table, which pocket it falls into, how many squares the ball has to cross.

Can you make any general statements?

Copymaster 80

Name _____

Level 5: Shape, space & measures

Networks (1 of 2)

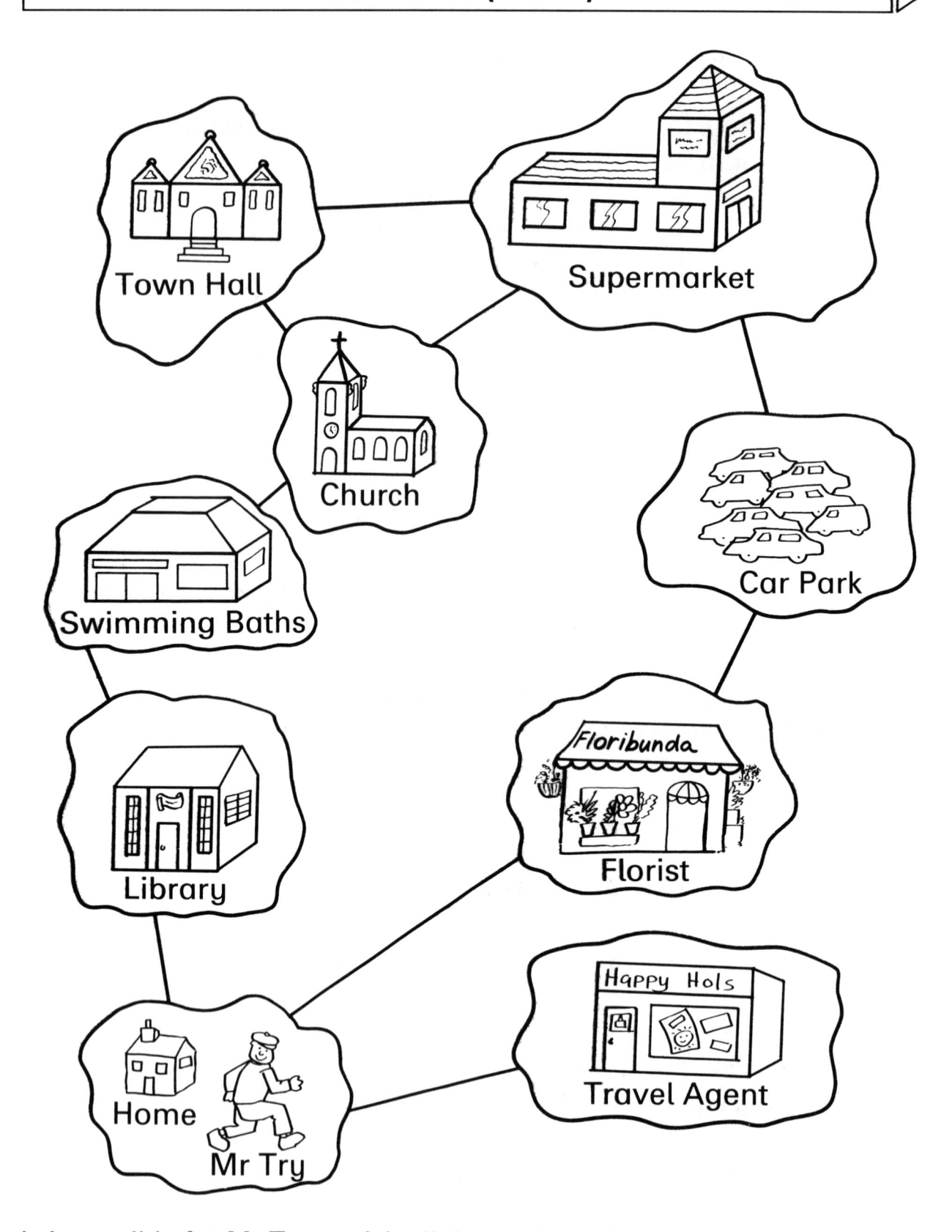

Town Hall

Supermarket

Church

Car Park

Swimming Baths

Library

Florist (Floribunda)

Home / Mr Try

Travel Agent (Happy Hols)

Is it possible for Mr Try to visit all these places in town and return home using all the routes marked only once? If not, what ways could you make Mr Try's trip possible? Look at the number of routes leading out of each location.

Copymaster 81

Name _____   Level 5: Shape, space & measures

Networks (2 of 2)

A net is traversable when you use all the pathways but each only once.

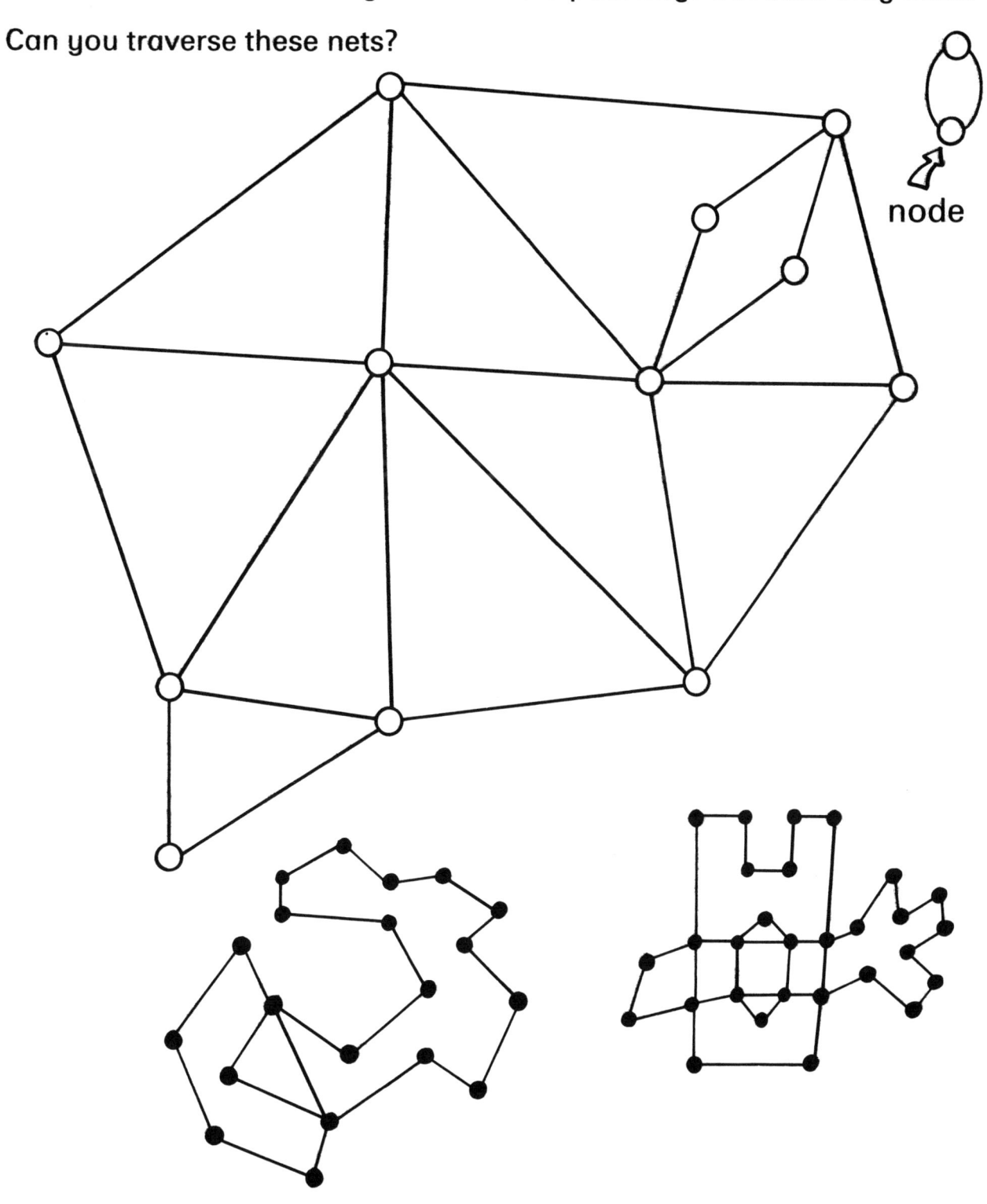

Can you traverse these nets?

← node

Does it matter where you start?

Does it matter where you aim to finish?

Look at the number of pathways coming out of each node. Draw some more networks to test your ideas.

Copymaster 82

Name _____

Level 5: Shape, space & measures

Knots

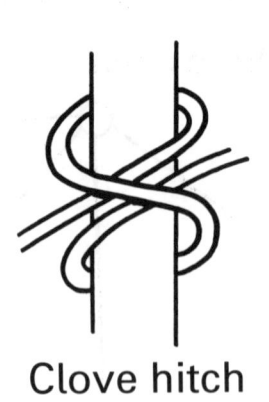

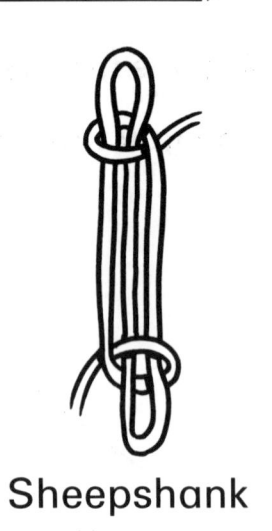

Overhand knot

Slipknot

Clove hitch

Sheepshank

Use a piece of string or wool to make these knots.

Draw a series of diagrams to show how to make two of them.

Find out more about knots and who uses them.

Copymaster 83

Name _____

Level 5: Shape, space & measures

Celtic knots

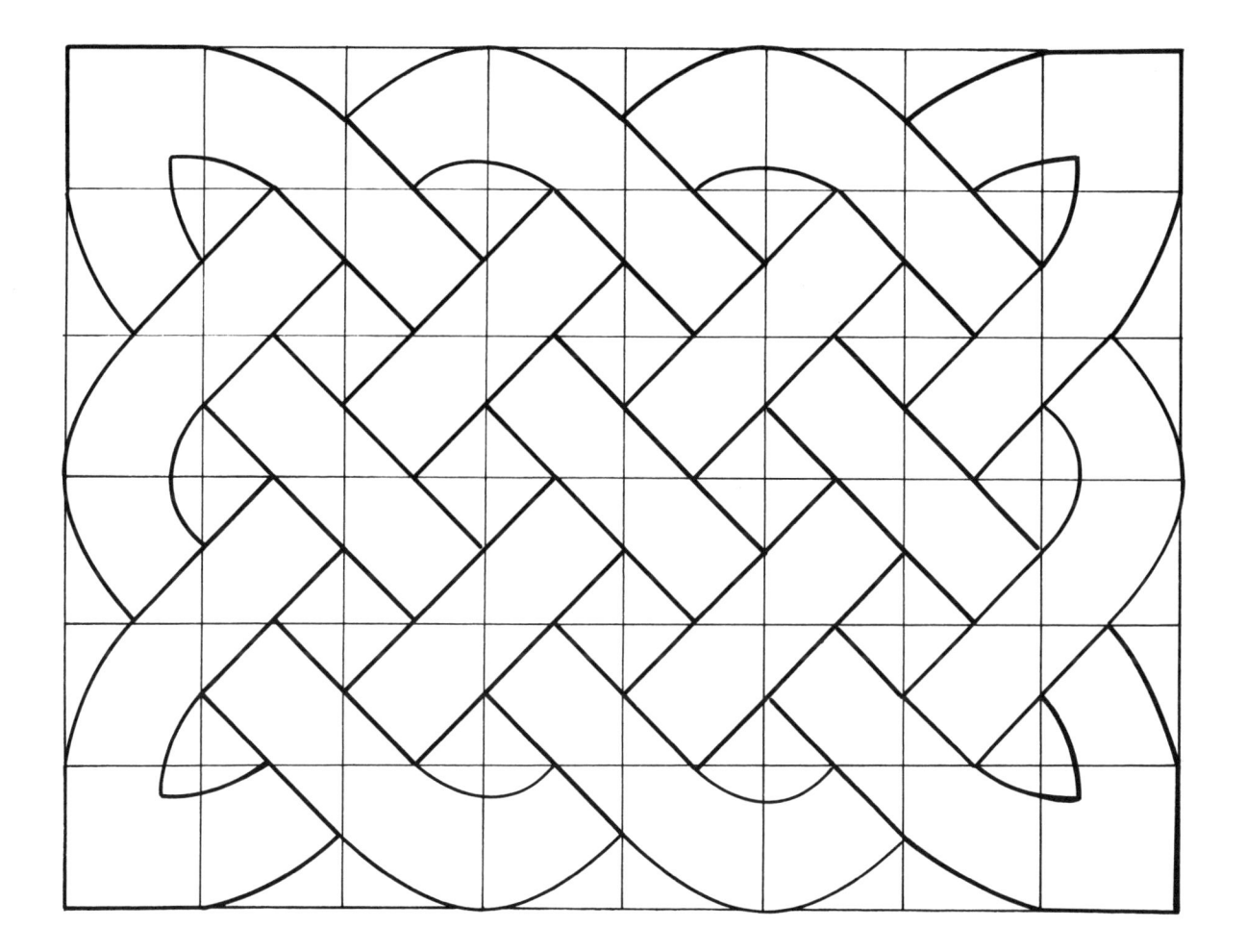

Using squared paper try making a copy of this knot. The basic idea is similar to that used in Celtic knots. Look for pictures of Celtic knots. Work out for each:
- How many strands are used?
- How many times does one strand cross another (or over itself)?
- How can the knot be drawn using squared paper?
- How many squares are needed?
- What size of square is best?

Draw a Celtic knot border to make a picture frame or book plate.

Copymaster 84

Name _____

Level 5: Shape, space & measures

Plaiting

Make a plait. Use three different colours. Draw what happens to each strand as you plait.

A B   C

Now try with more strands. How many 'moves' does each strand make before it gets back to the starting place?

Draw one of your plaits here.

1

2

3

4

5

6

Copymaster 85

Name _____

5 mm squared paper

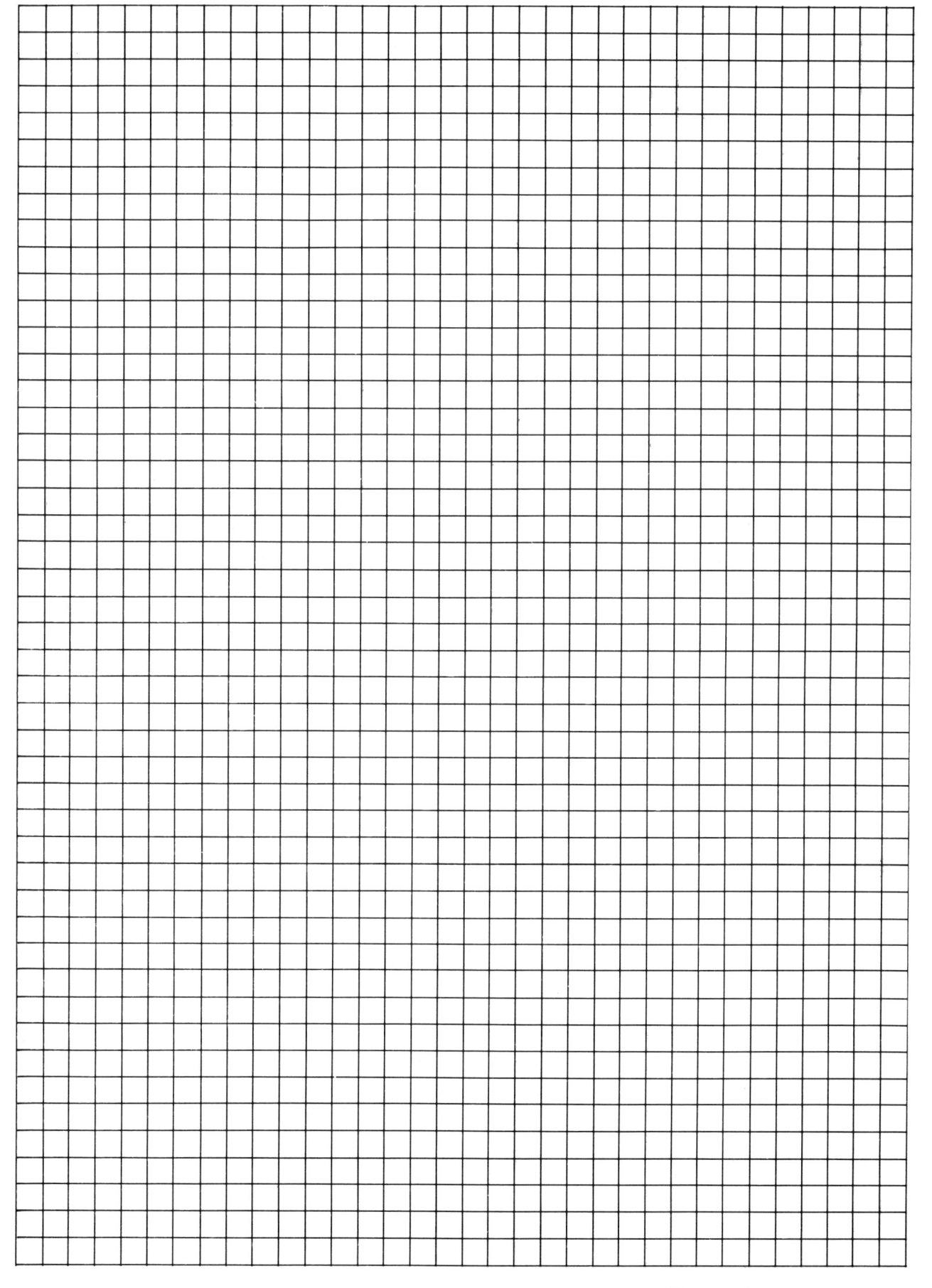

General copymaster a

Name _____

1 inch squared paper

General copymaster b

Name _____

1 cm squared paper

General copymaster c

Name _____

Triangle dotty paper

General copymaster d